Gracefully Broken

...Freedom from pain and generational curses through humility, inner healing and deliverance

By Yolanda Washington-Cowan

Unless otherwise indicated, scriptures are taken from the King James Version (KJV), New International Version (NIV), and Authorized King James Version (AKJV)

Gracefully Broken: Freedom from pain and curses through humility and inner healing

Copyright @ 2017 by Yolanda Washington-Cowan

All rights reserved

ISBN-13:978-0999777602
ISBN-10:0999777602

Published by

B-Inspired Publishing

7285 Winchester Road, Suite 109
Memphis, TN 38125

WWW.B-Inspiredpub.com

Printed in the United States

First Edition: December 2017

All rights reserved under International Copyright Law. Contents and/or cover may not be reproduced in whole or in part in any form without the expressed written consent of the Publisher.

*"God resists the proud,
but gives grace to the humble."*

This book is dedicated to my husband, son, mother and sisters, whom I adore and love with all my heart.

And all the Sisters on the 5a.m. and 7a.m. Prayer line.

ACKNOWLEDGEMENTS

I thank God for every tear that I have had to shed, all the bumps in the road that I have had to cross and every storm I've had to endure to get me to my ordained purpose and destiny. I love God with all my heart and soul. A special thanks to my husband for his insight and editing and our son for his assistance with the book cover. Also thanks to my Pastor for constantly feeding us with the word of God that encourages and inspires my family to live out our purpose and fulfill the Kingdom of God.

PREFACE

'Gracefully Broken' came from my personal struggle to reject the person I used to be and accept the person that God was leading me to become. It highlights the truths that I came to realize from the word of God as His Spirit gently led me from my past life.

I had come to a hard place in my life where I was caught between two options; to keep living in my familiar ways, even though the results were often negative, or to allow myself to be led into a new life which held a promise of happiness, in spite of its unfamiliarity.

As I've learned to humbly submit to God and obey Him, He led me on a journey that revealed things about me that I never knew. I gained new insights into why I did the things that I did, as the spiritual roots of my problems were exposed.

Through the word and power of God, I found deliverance from things that previously controlled me. And by constant prayer and fellowship with God's Holy Spirit, I not only found freedom from my past destructive lifestyle, but I also discovered the purpose of my life.

Sometimes in our lives, God has to break us to promote, position and bring us to our purpose. When he does this, it is not to destroy us; rather He does it gracefully, with a mind to help. I am a living witness of this, and I love God for breaking and bringing me to His plan and purpose for my life.

Using illustrations from my own experience, this book explains how you became the person that you are and uncovers the spiritual links between past generations of your family and your current situation. It shows you how to make a transition into a life of purpose and freedom.

By diligently reading and applying the truths inside these pages, your life will progress from a meaningless pursuit of things to a purposeful quest to become who you were created to be. You will discover insights that impart stability into your mind, your dreams and your relationships.

INTRODUCTION

What is going on in my life? Why do my relationships always fail? Why do I have so many financial issues? Why do I do the things that are wrong, when I know what is right? Why do bad things always happen to me? Why is God not answering my prayers? Maybe these are the questions you are asking yourself right now. You consider yourself a good person and probably attend church regularly, but your life has not reflected the promises of God. You are at a critical point where you feel that you can no longer go on in your own strength.

This book provides answers to some of the hardest questions people ask in the darkest moments of their lives. It gives an honest and scriptural perspective on the sources of the unsolvable issues in people's lives. Using a down-to-earth approach, it will guide you from struggling with difficulties you do not understand and set your feet on the path to power and freedom.

You will understand the spiritual and psychological forces that have been at work in your life since childhood; silent factors which have framed your current attitudes and results. The revelations you encounter in 'Gracefully Broken' are designed to help you discover the foundations of your everyday problems. Through it, you will take back full control of your life.

This book will help you offload the emotional burdens that have dogged your past life; results of negative events and relationships from yesterday. It will arm you with the tools to disconnect your destiny from your history, by showing you the emotional and spiritual doors that allow your life to be kept in a specific negative mode.

Using examples from my life and illustrations from the experiences of Biblical characters, you will understand how your current patterns of behavior are inherited from others rather than generated by you. And through the spiritual character of humility, you will learn how to apply the word of God to break all satanic oppressions from your life and experience God's fullness.

By the time you have reached the final chapter of this book, you would have acquired insight spanning many past generations of your family and gained valuable knowledge that will secure God's plan and purpose for your life. You will be freed from a life of self-will with its attendant troubles to a place of lasting peace and happiness in God.

I invite you to head on now to the first chapter and let us begin the journey!

CHAPTER ONE
BROKENNESS TO WHOLENESS

Have you ever come to a place in your walk with God, where it felt like you are engaged in a battle with Him? A place where it seemed as if you were wrestling with God over something in your life? The struggle might have been a step you wanted to take; it might have been about the ways you are accustomed to behaving, or beliefs you hold on to about other people or your attitude toward money. It might even be over the things that you felt you could never do because they were beneath you.

Whatever the source or reason for the struggle, such encounters deeply affect us. They unveil and threaten the very foundation of our lives; those things that are central to the way we have constructed our world. Through them we are forced to reexamine our identity, self-image, relationships, dreams and aspirations. And since these things are at the core of our being, making any form of adjustment in those areas feels like we are losing a part of ourselves; sometimes it even feels like dying.

Struggles like these determine the direction of our spiritual journey and even our destiny because they can be so life transforming. Regardless of whether the struggle is about money, relationships, ambitions or attitudes, the underlying issue is always about who has control of our lives. God demands something from us that will bring our life under his direction. We recognize this and sense that in giving in on these apparently small issues, we are giving up control. This is why we resist and why the conflicts are hard on us.

Giving up control is never easy because life experiences teach us to believe that the only person we can really trust in life is ourselves. But when we come to God, we begin to confront the reality that the only person we should trust is God. Because our past decisions and actions have repeatedly proven to be wrong and most of our current problems stem from our past mistakes. But it is very hard to trust that somebody else can do better for us than we have done for ourselves, especially when we have never had people to demonstrate that to us.

Living in a world where the weak get exploited; where we have been used by people and have used other people in turn, we learn that the number one rule in life is to look out for ourselves. We also begin to subconsciously value money and power as the ultimate goals for life, because we identify them as the only instruments that can protect us from harm and gain us respect from people. These beliefs are imposed on us by the necessity to survive the environment we are in; therefore, any attempt to take them from us encounters fierce resistance.

That is the very thing that God attempts to do with us. Why does He do this? Because He loves us and sees through our bold exterior to the fears and hurts that lurk inside our hearts. God recognizes the fragility of the life that we have built for ourselves; he sees that the way we live is not sustainable in the long run. And that we are storing up heartbreak, failure, disappointment, and loneliness for ourselves in the future. Our Heavenly Father sees that when the storms – harsh realities of life – eventually hit, everything we have built will crumble.

> Therefore everyone who hears these words of mine and puts them into practice is like a wise man who built his house on the rock. The rain came down, the streams rose, and the winds blew and beat against that house; yet it did not fall, because it had its foundation on the rock. But everyone who hears these words of mine and does not put them into practice is like a foolish man who built his house on sand. The rain came down, the streams rose, and the winds blew and beat against that house, and it fell with a great crash. **Matthew 7: 24-27 (NIV)**

God is trying to save us from ourselves. His actions in asking us to surrender are designed to take our lives out of our own incomepetent hands and plant them on a secure foundation. He is trying to save us from wasting our lives; His most precious gift to us. Everything He does is motivated by one prime goal; to give us a future and hope. The problem is we do not understand this. And where God is attempting to help, we think He wants to hurt. Where He is trying to give, we see Him as taking. And where He is delivering us, we think He is depriving us.

But just as a father with his children, the Heavenly Father persists. Not out of indifference to our objections but because, like a human father, He knows that we are blinded by childishness and lack the ability to make right judgments. Our minds are not developed enough to tell the difference between good and bad, and we lack the foresight and patience to discern the ultimate consequences of our actions. Therefore, out of love, God has to help and protect us from ourselves.

> And have you completely forgotten this word of encouragement that addresses you as a father ad-

dresses his son? It says,

> "My son, do not make light of the Lord's discipline, and do not lose heart when he rebukes you, because the Lord disciplines the one he loves, and he chastens everyone he accepts as his son."
>
> Endure hardship as discipline; God is treating you as his children. For what children are not disciplined by their father? If you are not disciplined—and everyone undergoes discipline—then you are not legitimate, not true sons and daughters at all. Moreover, we have all had human fathers who disciplined us and we respected them for it. How much more should we submit to the Father of spirits and live! They disciplined us for a little while as they thought best; but God disciplines us for our good, in order that we may share in his holiness. No discipline seems pleasant at the time, but painful. Later on, however, it produces a harvest of righteousness and peace for those who have been trained by it.
> **Hebrews 12:5-11 (NIV)**

Episodes of Divine reproof and correction are intended to achieve four important objectives:

They demonstrate God's love to His children. Although it might not be initially visible, later we can look back and realize that it had all been for our good.

They give Him the opportunity to bless us because God cannot bless us in pride, rebellion, and disobedience. When we submit to His will, we open the door to His blessings.

They secure God's purpose. There is a reason God created and saved us. Following His direction ensures that this purpose is fulfilled.

They give God glory. Our wrong ways of thinking and living dishonor God, because they do not give a positive testimony to the world. But when we become obedient, then the world can see his character correctly reflected through us.

And the number of years a person has been in church does not prevent them from an experience of Divine discipline. Our pedigree as choristers, committee members, youth leaders, Sunday school teachers, bible study teachers or whatever our position may be in the church does not give us immunity. As a matter of fact, it can be the reason why the process takes even longer and is harder. Because church people often have their true selves hidden behind a carefully crafted public image and letting God pierce through that pride and reputation takes a lot. We will examine Jacob as a practical example of someone going through a season of Divine correction.

Jacob's Struggles

Jacob had pedigree; he was Abraham's grandson. And before His birth, God had spoken a prophetic word over his life assuring him of God's blessing in his life. But Jacob had a problem, the blessing God promised would normally be given to the firstborn son of the house, and that was his brother. So Jacob construed to have his older brother, Esau, give up his birthright to him, making Jacob the official holder of the position of the firstborn. But there was another problem; their father didn't know about it or chose to ignore it.

Eventually, the day came when his father would confer the blessing on his sons based on order of birth; the day Jacob had been waiting for. Jacob's father, Isaac, instructed his older brother, Esau, to go hunt deer and make a spicy soup of venison for him. His father wanted this because it would lift his spirit and enable him to bless Esau. Jacob was absent when his father gave Esau the instruction, but he had an ally in his mother, Rebecca.

Rebecca overheard the conversation between her first son and her husband, and she informed Jacob her favorite son, also advising him what to do. So Jacob, along with his mother, fooled his blind father into believing that he was Esau and blessing him in Esau's place. Thus, Jacob was able to obtain the blessing that God had originally promised him before he was born, although through deception. But there was yet another problem; Esau understandably angry, decided to kill Jacob. That was a huge problem because Esau was a warrior and Jacob was a shepherd.

So Jacob, on his mother's advice, fled. And since he had no other place to go, his mother sent him to Haran, where she was originally from and where her brother still lived. But by going to Haran, Jacob effectively endangered his chances of ever getting the blessing he had been chasing. Though his grandfather, Abraham, came from Haran to Canaan, he promised God that neither he nor his children would ever return there. But Jacob did. As a result of his craftiness and unbridled pursuit of things, Jacob trapped himself into going to a place where God's grace couldn't fully cover him.

But God didn't abandon him. He recognized that Jacob, like many of his children, had weaknesses that prevented them from doing the right things. He saw Jacob's desire to be God's instrument even though his motives were wrong and his methods ungodly. Beyond his actions, God looked to his heart and decided to help him. He had a choice to abandon Jacob to the consequences of his actions; a life of failure in Haran. Rather, after twenty years, He intervened and delivered Jacob.

> So Jacob was left alone, and a man wrestled with him till daybreak. When the man saw that he could not overpower him, he touched the socket of Jacob's hip so that his hip was wrenched as he wrestled with the man. Then the man said, "Let me go, for it is daybreak." But Jacob replied, "I will not let you go unless you bless me." The man asked him, "What is your name?" "Jacob," he answered. Then the man said, "Your name will no longer be Jacob, but Israel, because you have struggled with God and with humans and have overcome." Jacob said, "Please tell me your name." But he replied, "Why do you ask my name?" Then he blessed him there. So Jacob called the place Peniel, saying, "It is because I saw God face to face, and yet my life was spared." The sun rose above him as he passed Peniel, and he was limping because of his hip. Therefore to this day the Israelites do not eat the tendon attached to the socket of the hip, because the socket of Jacob's hip was touched near the tendon. **Gens 32:24-32 (NIV)**

In the verse above, Jacob had just escaped from Haran and was on his way to Canaan when he received news that Esau was on his way to meet him with an army. Here he was, trying to recover from one mistake when he comes face-to-face with an even worse one. How would he handle the situation? As we often do, Jacob resorted to his usual tried-and-tested way of handling difficulties; manipulating people. Yet he realized that this time, it would not be enough. So he did what he had never done before, he prayed. For the first time in his life, Jacob asks the help of the One whose blessings he had been asking all these years.

Like Jacob you may have come to a place where you can no longer go forward. After having tried tricks that succeeded in the past, without success, you turn to God with desperation. Such times force us as believers to give God complete attention. Because we are at our wit's end, we are ready for a renegotiation of terms and to accept God's terms for His continued involvement in our lives. We are desperate enough to listen, surrender and change. These situations are God's opportunities to get us to listen and to change the course of our lives.

Although what Jacob was trying to escape was the consequence of his own deceit, his prayer was not repentance. Jacob asked God to bless him; believing that God's blessing would somehow overshadow his lack of character. He could go on living as he always had, while enjoying the approval of God. He wasn't concerned with the root of the problem, only with the pain. He wanted God to help him not change him. But until he saw who he really was, he would continue acting in ways that would sabotage any blessing God brought into his Life. This is the reason God had to wrestle with him; to humble him until he surrenders, listened and changed.

Jacob's story is the story of our lives; our experiences almost always follow the same path as his did.

Pain

We never pay attention until we find ourselves in a difficult situation. Our 'smart ways' and 'sharp practices' have complicated our lives and brought us into a place where we are in danger of losing our minds, families, finances, property, businesses, health and even our lives. Faced with this reality, we finally humble ourselves enough to seek God's presence. It finally enters our consciousness that maybe God has something to offer that could change our situation. But even in this state, we are not praying to change our ways but merely looking for a way to use God as we have used people.

> Some sat in darkness, in utter darkness, prisoners suffering in iron chains, because they rebelled against God's commands and despised the plans of the Most High. So he subjected them to bitter labor; they stumbled, and there was no one to help. Then they cried to the Lord in their trouble, and he saved them from their distress. He brought them out of darkness, the utter darkness, and broke away their chains. **Psalm 107: 10-14 (NIV)**

Self-Righteousness

And like Jacob, the focus of our prayer is ourselves. We feel justified in our actions and question why the things that have happened to us happened. We never think to discover the cause or source of our troubles. And if we ever do, we tend to blame God, our spouse, parents, children and even the church. Everyone gets blamed but ourselves. And even if we accept that we did do some things wrong, we feel justified in how we acted because of how other people acted. We are self-righteous. But

God will only work for us when He is able to bring us to the place of humility and repentance.

> If my people, who are called by my name, will humble themselves and pray and seek my face and turn from their wicked ways, then I will hear from heaven, and I will forgive their sin and will heal their land. **2 Chronicles 7:14 (NIV)**

Refocus

Throughout the encounter, God works to refocus our attention away from receiving his blessing and blaming others, to finally considering if perhaps there could be another way to view the issues. He gets us to begin to see things differently, beginning with how we see ourselves. We are stripped naked in His presence and see ourselves, warts, scars and all. Then we see our exact role in the events of our lives and begin to realize that we are not the saint we have deluded ourselves into believing. This revelation can feel like an emotional earthquake, and its effect is such that we do not think we can go on with life because we instinctively realize that we cannot continue being the person we used to be.

> For God does speak - now one way, now another- though no one perceives it. In a dream, in a vision of the night, when deep sleep falls on people as they slumber in their beds, he may speak in their ears and terrify them with warnings, to turn them from wrongdoing and keep them from pride. **Job 33: 14-17 (NIV)**

> But who can discern their own errors? Forgive my hidden faults. Keep your servant also from willful

sins (Or sins of presumption); may they not rule over me. Then I will be blameless, innocent of great transgression. May these words of my mouth and this meditation of my heart be pleasing in your sight, Lord, my Rock and my Redeemer. **Psalm 19: 12-14 (NIV)**

Hope

The Holy Spirit is called our comforter, and it is at such times that we begin to really experience this. Just as God led Jacob until he saw himself as the schemer he was, and then He began to show him who he could be, God does the same with us. The reason He takes us into the place of prayer and self-revelation is not so that he can condemn us but to give us an opportunity to change. And we cannot change until we recognize the problem. When we see ourselves and repent in 'sackcloth and ashes,' the Spirit of God begins to show us new ways of living, and our heart begins to open to new opportunities for future blessing.

> But if people are bound in chains, held fast by cords of affliction, he tells them what they have done - that they have sinned arrogantly. He makes them listen to correction and commands them to repent of their evil. If they obey and serve him, they will spend the rest of their days in prosperity and their years in contentment. **Job 36:8-12 (NIV)**

Healing and Transformation

Finally, the experience results in windows of spiritual, emotional, and relationship healing. We have come to the place of surrender and malleability. We become plaster in the potter's hands, and he can mold us into the shape that he wants us to take. We enter into a time of spiritual childhood, as we abandon our old ways and begin to slowly learn the ways of God as we discover different ways to approach the old situations in our lives. We become broken and start to be transformed. Broken from our hardened, obstinate and inflexible self which did not yield to God but was fixed on its own ways, to a new person who is willing to give way to the voice and commands of God's word. Our point of view is changed.

> Before I was afflicted I went astray, but now I obey your word. You are good, and what You do is good; teach me your decrees. Though the arrogant have smeared me with lies, I keep your precepts with all my heart. Their hearts are callous and unfeeling, but I delight in your law. It was good for me to be afflicted so that I might learn your decrees. The law from your mouth is more precious to me than thousands of pieces of silver and gold. **Psalm 119:67-72 (NIV)**

Experiences like these are the tools that God uses to break His children. Breaking in this regard does not mean destruction but transformation. Before we come to God, we have become fixed in the ways that we viewed life, treated people, related to money and in what we considered as the most important things in life. Every one of us had preconceived notions that continued to guide us even after we had become believers. And these ideas did not always align with God's word. But God brings us through brokenness so that His word will become our highest treasure and the guiding light of our lives.

CHAPTER TWO

SURRENDERING TO GOD

How did you become the way that you are? A person's ability to correctly answer this question unveils the powers at work within their lives. By understanding the sources of our behavior, we uncover the forces that we struggle against. Everyone one of us has a history that goes beyond our oldest memories of ourselves. Sometimes to reach the destination, we might need to go back 100 years in our generation. Before you became the person you recognize yourself to be, there were forces acting in your life. Those forces framed the person you eventually call you.

Our inability to see the root of the problem is itself the problem. While we are trying to solve the immediate problems of finance, relationships, work, health, etc., God is working to solve the real problem that creates these other ones. Everything you are dealing with today began long before you ever encountered anything connected with the issue. Relationship problems began before we had our first relationship. Money problems began before we earned our first dollar. Spiritual problems began before we came to God.

We all come to God twisted and bent out of shape from whatever places we are coming from. And not only are we spiritually deformed or malformed, we have also become hardened in place. Any attempt to reshape us results in pain; but just like a bone fracture that did not heal properly, the only way to repair us is to break us. Doing so causes pain and reopens the old wound, but it also provides new opportunities for healing. If this is not done, the bone gets progressively twisted out of shape until the person can no longer stand upright or walk straight.

Everything that we struggle with has a pattern. There is a pattern to our sexual behavior. There is a pattern to our financial behavior. There is a pattern to the kind of people we choose as friends. There is a pattern to the ways we behave when confronted with problems. There is a pattern to our response to authority. There is a pattern to our moods and emotions. These patterns reveal underlying beliefs, attitudes and memories. The fact is that, most of the time; you and I are not responding to life on the basis of the realities of a situation but according to the rule book inside our heads that we subconsciously consult.

How Our Hearts Are Framed: The Example of Jacob

In the case of Jacob, there was also a pattern.

> Even from birth the wicked go astray; from the womb they are wayward, spreading lies. Their venom is like the venom of a snake, like that of a cobra that has stopped its ears, that will not heed the tune of the charmer, however skillful the enchanter may be. **Psalm 58:3-5 (NIV)**

Many years before Jacob's Father, Isaac, was born, his grandfather Abraham went to Egypt to escape a famine in Canaan. While over there, the Egyptian King spotted Sarah, Jacob's grandmother and took her into his harem because when he asked her, she said Abraham was her brother. It took God's intervention to get Sarah out untouched. One year before the birth of

Isaac, Abraham went to Gerar to escape a famine and did the same thing. The King of Gerar took Sarah into his harem and God had to step in once more to free Sarah.

All this happened before Jacob's father, Isaac, was born. Yet over forty years after Abraham went to Gerar, Isaac also went to Gerar to escape a famine and he repeated the exact same pattern of behavior as his father. He and his wife, Rebecca, told everyone that they were siblings. But this time around, Rebecca was spared the shame of being taken into another man's house because someone spotted them cuddling in secret and reported the matter to the King.

This pattern of behavior reveals a system of thinking. Jacob came from a family line where the men could resort to deceit to escape a difficult situation, even at the risk of destroying their most important relationships, family. Admittedly, they acted like this only in difficult situations but it did not lessen the enormity or impact of their actions. Few men would allow another man to sleep with their girlfriends, much less their wives. Even more interesting is the kind of woman who would accept to cooperate with her husband in acting like that.

These men came from a cultural background where a man could use his wife or daughter's sexual favors to secure an economic or political advantage from another man. In turn, the women got used to their men's insensitivity and became emotionally scarred; treating their relationships as mere financial transactions. Marriages lost intimacy, as a result, and became contracts. The man used his wife to gain power and she, in turn, leveraged the children to control and punish him. By intervening to save Sarah, God was trying to save Abraham and Isaac from the ways of their ancestors.

Jacob was born and raised up in this environment. His father, Isaac, refused to deal with the contentious issue of the prophecy about the blessing. He refused to deal with Esau's wayward behavior because of what he got from him. And since the head of the home did not provide leadership or impose order, everyone in his house resorted to living as they saw fit. What mattered to them was to get whatever they wanted, regardless of how they got it and who got hurt in the process.

Additionally, Jacob was named Trickster; a name he would not have wanted but which he came to accept. Because people can repeatedly tell you who they think you are until your spirit succumbs and you not only accept their opinion but start living up to their expectations. Words from authority figures in our young age can become a self-fulfilling prophecy. When children are regularly exposed to stress that is not resolved for them by the adults in their lives, they develop coping mechanisms which could be to ignore the situation, to manipulate people, to become aggressive or to fawn.

These issues lay at the heart of Jacob's previous way of life. But if God merely told him to stop behaving in a certain way, he would only be changing Jacob's outward actions and not his heart. The real challenge was to expose Jacob to the true condition of his spirit. Merely telling him that he had swindled his brother was not difficult. That much Jacob knew already; that is why he employed various gifts and tricks to try and appease Esau. The real struggle was to show Jacob that he was not just called Jacob, he had actually become Jacob. He did not just use, trickery; he was now a Trickster.

This is always the case with people; we like to believe that we behave in the ways that we do by choice. Although we have become addicted to those thoughts and actions, we insist that we can change whenever we choose. The truth, though, is that at one point it might have been a choice and within our power to control, but now it has become a habit that we are enslaved to. That way of life has become the default mode of our mind; the first and most attractive option we ever consider. It is now the course that we follow intuitively because we experience the least internal resistance acting that way.

So, the first struggle is for God to even bring us to the place where we can see who we really are. The next struggle is to have us accept that we have become slaves of those thoughts and emotions. And finally, God wrestles with us to disprove our excuses and attempts to justify our behavior, and instead have us repent of them unconditionally. When confronted with our true selves, we rationalize our actions by blaming people and circumstances or claiming that we were weak and deserved to be pitied. But until we acknowledge our actions to be wrong, we cannot gain access to God's mercy and the Grace which enables us to break free.

Uncovering the Spring of Your Life

> So I tell you this, and insist on it in the Lord, that you must no longer live as the Gentiles do, in the futility of their thinking. They are darkened in their understanding and separated from the life of God because of the ignorance that is in them due to the hardening of their hearts. Having lost all sensitivity, they have given themselves over to sensuality so as to indulge in every kind of impurity, and they are full of greed. **Ephesians 4:17-19 (NIV)**

> The god of this age has blinded the minds of unbelievers, so that they cannot see the light of the gospel that displays the glory of Christ, who is the image of God. 2 **Corinthians 4:4 (NIV)**

When we realize that the ways we think and behave did not happen by chance but are the results of a satanic strategy to derail our destinies, we start to recognize the value of submitting to God. The devil knows that the human soul is formed in our young age, and that once formed we go forward acting according to the contents of our hearts, hardly questioning our beliefs. The experiences of our young lives form the basis upon which we build our whole lives. Most of what people learn after their formative years are merely intellectual or they just reinforce the ideas that we have already formed about life.

This is why Satan goes after young people and families. He understands that the home is the mold which frames the heart of a child. And if he can break or fracture the home, the children it produces will inherit the same dysfunctions as their parents inside their spirits. They will go through life living according to the shape into which they have been bent. And when those children have their own children, they will use the same broken molds to frame their children's spirit and make them just like the parents. This becomes a self-perpetuating cycle or what the Bible calls, a generational curse.

This is the reason some children inexplicably repeat the negative thought patterns, impulses, decisions, choices and results of their parents. And the process can go on for hundreds of years, until the curse becomes so normalized that people accept it as the way things are supposed to be.

> Above all else, guard your heart, for everything you do flows from it. **Proverbs 4:23 (NIV)**

> For with you is the fountain of life; in your light we see light. **Psalm 36:9 (NIV)**

Our hearts can be affected in such a way that it supplies a constant stream of bitter experiences. We notice the effect of that impaired heart but do not realize its source. But as we fellowship with God, He brings us into a place in His presence where his Spirit can illuminate our hearts and awaken us to the processes at work within ourselves. We come to the realization of our own self-destructive ways and yield ourselves to His control, so that His spirit can reach into us and uproot the tree of sin, depravity and misconduct. But before this can begin we must surrender ourselves to God.

> I will give you a new heart and put a new spirit in you; I will remove from you your heart of stone and give you a heart of flesh. **Ezekiel 36:26 (NIV)**

Just like a stone which is unyielding and unfeeling, our hearts used to be unresponsive to the word of God and the needs of other people. We were dominated by our own selfish ways. We hurt others, just as they hurt us, until our lives were filled with senseless pain, hate and anger. In spite of it all, we did not change, because we could not see any need to. Our stony hearts would not allow us to hear or listen to others' point of view; we were always right, we had to be. But God's word in the verse above promises to change our hearts. He says that He will deliver us from the fixed ways in which we had previously lived.

> If my people, who are called by my name, will humble themselves and pray and seek my face and

> turn from their wicked ways, then I will hear from heaven, and I will forgive their sin and will heal their land. **2 Chronicles 7:14 (NIV)**

But this promise hinges on humility.

Giving Up Control

And humility involves surrendering. Surrender is not a song people sing in church or about responding to an altar call. Surrendering means to hand over control of the key decision points of our lives to God. This means that the strategic thoughts, emotions, choices, actions and relationships that have so far determined the course of our lives are given over to God. So that He now holds the compass that gives us orientation. He holds decision making powers over those things that establish our identity and destiny. When we surrender we give up government of our lives and make God our King. His word becomes the law guiding our every conduct.

Surrender opens the door for us to change. Surrendering does not mean change but it creates the chance for change to happen. Because through surrendering we come to acknowledge our current points of views, choices and relationships as wrong. Without this acknowledgment, God cannot work in our lives; if He attempted to, He would be subverting our will. The Spirit of God does not want to break into your house and begin to rearrange your furniture. Rather, He asks you to hand over the front door keys, the keys to other rooms and closets, as well as passwords to every device. Surrendering has the effect of giving God unfettered access into our lives. We become naked, as nothing is hidden from the searchlight of His word.

> Search me, God, and know my heart; test me and know my anxious thoughts. See if there is any offensive way in me, and lead me in the way everlasting.
> **Psalm 139:23-24 (NIV)**

The Promise of Grace

Surrendering to God's will open windows for seasons of change to enter our lives. By saying YES, we create the environment of willingness necessary for God's Grace, the vehicle of His power, to function and change us. But sometimes believers struggle with surrendering because they are preoccupied with thinking about how much effort changing will demand of them. They hold back on the urge to say 'Yes Lord!' because they fear that they may not be able to follow through on their commitment. But changing yourself is not your job. Your responsibility is to accept God's ways, acknowledge your faults and permit God's Spirit to work in you.

> "No one can come to me unless the Father who sent me draws them, and I will raise them up at the last day. **John 6:44 (NIV)**

> Blessed are those you choose and bring near to live in your courts! We are filled with the good things of your house, of your holy temple. **Psalm 65:4 (NIV)**

> I have seen his ways, and will heal him: I will lead him also, and restore comforts unto him and to his mourners. I create the fruit of the lips; Peace, peace to him that is far off, and to him that is near, saith the Lord; and I will heal him. **Isaiah 57:18-19 (AKJV)**

The fact that we are even able to contemplate the Word of God and consider giving in to His will comes from God. To think that after He has brought us to the place of awakening, we can now accomplish His will by our own strength, is an error. God supplies the ingredient needed to transform the stony heart to a fleshly one. He provides the fire, we bring the sacrifice. We surrender, but God changes. We offer ourselves and the fire of His spirit consumes the filth and refines the gold in us. As long as we hold the view that we are the ones who need to change ourselves, we are still locked in our past mode of thinking. The power to change us lies with God, so that the glory can also belong to Him.

> For it is God who works in you to will and to act in order to fulfill his good purpose. **Philippians 2:13 (NIV)**

Growing In The Lord

> For this very reason, make every effort to add to your faith goodness; and to goodness, knowledge; and to knowledge, self-control; and to self-control, perseverance; and to perseverance, godliness; and to godliness, mutual affection; and to mutual affection, and love. For if you possess these qualities in increasing measure, they will keep you from being ineffective and unproductive in your knowledge of our Lord Jesus Christ. But whoever does not have them is nearsighted and blind, forgetting that they have been cleansed from their past sins. **2 Peter 1:5-9 (NIV)**

Surrendering is progressive; it does not occur in one night of encounter. If our lives were a political kingdom, surrendering would mean handing over the seat of government to a new king. But that would not mean that every home, village, town and city in the country now lived by the laws of the new king. There would be places where people kept living as they had always done. However, as the new administration gets established, the new king's officials would begin to encounter incidents of nonconformance as they spread through the land. Slowly, but surely, they would eventually bring the whole country under the dominion of the new king. That is also how surrender works in our lives too.

Our initial surrendering experience hands control of the dominant and highly visible aspects of our lives to God. Those are the key aspects that clearly indicate that our lives have been given over to the Lord. But as we walk with God, and His Spirit walks through our spirits, things in our lives which do not agree with our declared intention to serve God begin to show up and He demands surrender in those areas too. This progressive act of surrendering is what we term as SPIRITUAL GROWTH and it is fundamental in creating the new person that we are becoming.

This process of surrendering occurs on different levels and dimension of our lives. The goal of the Holy Spirit's is to make us unrecognizable in character from the person that we were framed to become as a result of life experiences. Rather than be ruled by impulses, emotions and lusts, God is building us into a person who subjects themselves to the higher principles of His truth. From living carelessly, we go to living an examined life.

> And we all, who with unveiled faces contemplate the Lord's glory, are being transformed into his image with ever-increasing glory, which comes from the Lord, who is the Spirit. **2 Corinthians 3:18 (NIV)**

Our surrender to God is reflected on these various levels:

Intellectual Surrender

> And because I consider all your precepts right, I hate every wrong path. Your statutes are wonderful; therefore I obey them. **Psalm 119:128-129 (NIV)**

> Your word is a lamp for my feet, a light on my path. **Psalm 119:105 (NIV)**

The ideas we hold are no longer drawn from the surrounding culture of greed, pleasure-seeking, selfishness, violence, insensitivity, un spirituality, etc. The word of God becomes the reference point in the values, beliefs and opinions that we hold. Where there is disagreement between what we have always believed and what the word of God says, God's word wins.

Directional Surrender

> Whoever serves me must follow me; and where I am, my servant also will be. My Father will honor the one who serves me. **John 12:26 (NIV)**

> For none of us lives for ourselves alone, and none of us dies for ourselves alone. If we live, we live for the Lord; and if we die, we die for the Lord. So, whether we live or die, we belong to the Lord. **Romans 14:7-8 (NIV)**

Our purpose and the direction of our lives are controlled by what God tells us. We invest our energies, time and resources for his glory. Our gifts and abilities are offered back to him.

Relational Surrender

> Do not be yoked together with unbelievers. For what do righteousness and wickedness have in common? Or what fellowship can light have with darkness? What harmony is there between Christ and Belial? Or what does a believer have in common with an unbeliever? **2 Corinthians 6:14-15 (NIV)**

We surrender our hearts to God and make him Lord of our emotions; permitting ourselves to love only those who love Him. This doesn't mean that we do not relate to non-believers. But it means that those intimate relationships and personal spaces which influence who we become are only open to those who hold the values as we do.

Material Surrender

> Accept instruction from his mouth and lay up his words in your heart. If you return to the Almighty, you will be restored: If you remove wickedness far from your tent and assign your nuggets to the dust, your gold of Ophir to the rocks in the ravines, then the Almighty will be your gold, the choicest silver for you. **Job 22:22-25 (NIV)**

> Honor the Lord with your wealth, with the first fruits of all your crops; then your barns will be filled to

> overflowing, and your vats will brim over with new wine. **Proverbs 3:9-10 (NIV)**

We become stewards of the material resources in our hands. And recognize that everything is held in trust for God's purpose and that not just our tithes but our treasures belong to God. As such, we will give Him account for how we spent the money He gave into our hands.

Why We Struggle to Surrender

> Very truly I tell you, when you were younger you dressed yourself and went where you wanted; but when you are old you will stretch out your hands, and someone else will dress you and lead you where you do not want to go." **John 21:18 (NIV)**

Giving in to God's Word is a struggle because we fear that it means we have lost the chance of gaining those things that we pursued. We somehow feel that if we gave up that relationship, we are giving up any chance of future happiness. We feel that if we give up the unbridled pursuit of money, we would never succeed. We fear that if we became less arrogant, selfish and contentious, there would be no way to protect ourselves and people would take us for fools.

The reason we feel this way is because that is the only way we know to live. We have never seen anyone become successful without being dishonest and manipulative. We have never seen a relationship that is not built on mutual selfishness, where each party is not just out to meet their own needs. We have never realized that it takes more power to refrain from violent and abusive behavior. And that people who are violent only confirm the very thing they are trying to escape, their own weakness. Our assumptions about life are drawn from our limited terms of reference.

As a result, surrender feels very much like dying. It is as though we are emptied out of all hope and aspiration. This is only normal because those dreams were linked to our ways of thinking. We believed we could find love because we were seductive. We believed we could succeed because we were skillful at manipulation. We thought we could be happy because we owned the best things. So naturally, when we could no longer be seductive, manipulative or materialistic, we also stopped believing that we could be loved, successful or happy.

And letting go of those things is very important because once we have been able to say NO, it becomes easier to say it again and again. If we indulge a desire, it gets stronger. If we deny it, it gets weaker. By bringing us to the place of letting go, God builds resilience and strength into us. Moreover, it causes things to lose their hold on us, even legitimate things. We are no longer enslaved to the idea of happiness, love and success. We see them as blessings that enrich our lives rather than the reason for our lives.

> But seek first his kingdom and his righteousness,
> and all these things will be given to you as well.
> **Matthew 6:33 (NIV)**

© ChristinLola www.fotosearch.com

INTERLUDE ONE: MY STORY

Brokenness and Conflict

I grew up in poverty, but always had the basic necessities to live. I was raised by a single mother who worked a lot; she worked in many factories and part-time at a diner. My mother worked so much that as a young child, I grew up between many family members' houses. I had almost no relationship with my father until I became a teenager. I am the oldest of three siblings.

As a young child growing up in the inner city, on a daily basis, I saw prostitution, gambling behind dumpsters in the alleys, fighting, shooting, dope pushers, drug & alcoholic addiction, a family of ten trying to survive in a one-bedroom home, fathers against sons, mothers against daughters, blue-collar workers struggling to raise a family of five or more on minimum wage, extramarital affairs, lying, stealing, and the list goes on.

I wore borrowed clothes and had to eat at other people's tables. There were days I would go to school or church and see other children with the best of things, and then I would daydream that if I made the right choices, I, too, could have those things. I never ever wanted to have to borrow somebody else's clothes, shoes, or beg anyone for anything again in my life. I realized at an early age that what I saw growing up was not a lifestyle I wanted in my future. So, I made a choice to want more out of life; I chose prosperity over poverty.

I was determined to beat the poverty mindset mentality and escape the streets. But looking back, I believe that this period of my life was when I gave the enemy legal grounds for specific evil spirits to enter my life. Spirits of selfishness, defensiveness, self-sufficiency (I can do it all by myself), self-aspirations (over-competitiveness), self-seeking (It's all about me), Jezebel spirit (controlling), disobedience and pride found an opening into my life.

I started working at an early age; for one dime I ran to the corner grocery store for seniors in the neighborhood and I cleaned houses on weekends for a dollar and fifty cents. I was the local paper girl and I picked up aluminum cans and sold them at one dollar for a 10-pound bag. By the time I reached my senior year, I was working two jobs and missed a lot of high-school class events because I had to work. For me, it was all about getting my money and building something for myself. I just worked and worked determinedly to break the curse of poverty.

I had always been in church all my life; I think I received my salvation when I was twelve. I attended a traditional Baptist church for thirty years, where I was getting fed the traditional word. Although I went to church faithfully, I was still living in sin. I lived in sin for so long it became a part of my life; to the point where I thought it was right. I came and went, heard the Word of God but always returned to doing the same things. I let myself get spiritually robbed by being in a church where I didn't grow, and my mind was not being conformed to God's word.

In a traditional church, they normally didn't teach inner healing and deliverance. So I lived by what I saw, my choices were made in the flesh and according to the generational curses in my life. At that time, I didn't know about generational curses or the reasons for the pattern of things in my life. But I do not fault anybody for this; I fault myself because I did not want more, I did not reach out to learn more about the gifts that God had for me. Being stuck in a church that teaches traditional things often gives the enemy the advantage over us by allowing him to keep us ignorant of all spiritual gifts and our authority in Christ.

And my ignorance led me to sin. I made bad choices and responded to situations the way I should never have; totally out of character. When I finally recognized this, I had to apologize to God for not being more knowledgeable of his word and for not wanting more of him. I got into my first marriage when I was very young. We were two young people who were really broken from childhood but did not have the spiritual awareness to realize that we were spiritually and psychologically damaged and needed inner healing and deliverance. He sinned and I sinned, and the marriage eventually ended in divorce.

Later on, however, I came to realize that one sin was no better than the other. When I recognized that I was just as wrong as he was and understood that I had to repent, I went to my first husband and we both repented and asked forgiveness of each other. We defeated the devil by letting go of the past. Asking the other person for forgiveness brings humility and I learned in that process that it was okay to admit that I was wrong and to apologize. Later in our lives, we also both realized that the act of forgiving brought about inner healing into our hearts and released the blessings that God has for us. We are both happily married to other people.

I had to be broken to do this; the storms and struggles that I had encountered in my life showed me how broken I was from childhood to adulthood. I had hidden that brokenness behind work and all the material stuff I had acquired, but I was still messed up deep inside. I arrived at a point in my life where I was emotionally, physically and mentally drained from always having to fight; struggling for stuff, fighting with people, and constantly insisting on my own way. I needed inner healing and deliverance to be made whole and I knew the only source was God. I surrendered to God in humility and finally realized that His way is the best way. I just love God; for showing me myself in raw form.

CHAPTER THREE
CONFESSION AND REPENTANCE

Words are the currency of spiritual transactions. All human interactions are built on a foundation of words. The wedding ceremony is built upon the exchange of words or vows by the couple. The license only affirms that those words have been spoken. Some people will never set eyes on the license but firmly believe the couple to be married because they witnessed the exchange of words. Words frame the history of our personal relationships; the extent to which we relate to people depends on how much their words agree with our ideas of ourselves. We judge people by what they say and that is why we find liars so disturbing; they disrupt and attempt to subvert this natural and established process for determining relationships through the exchange of words.

Words form the basis of all contracts and agreements. Business agreements and work relationships only begin after the parties have talked. And until the discussions arrive at a common basis, the agreements are not concluded. Even afterward the contract does not create confidence in us, although it has been signed. What gives us confidence is the other party's trustworthiness; a history of how their past actions have aligned with their proclamations. Words give us insight into the nature of a person – a window into their souls. People are the totality of the words that they hold inside themselves, namely their thoughts. Words make up any person's essence. And words possess creative or destructive power.

The world originally sprang into existence through the Word that God spoke. And because words form the foundations of our universe, they continue to create and recreate our world.

> Through faith we understand that the worlds were framed by the word of God, so that things which are seen were not made of things which do appear. **Hebrews 11:3 (AKJV)**

This is why everything that God has ever given to humankind began with words or is based on words.

> The Lord had said to Abram, "Go from your country, your people and your father's household to the land I will show you. "I will make you into a great nation, and I will bless you; I will make your name great, and you will be a blessing. I will bless those who bless you, and whoever curses you I will curse; and all peoples on earth will be blessed through you."
> **Genesis 12:1-3 (NIV)**

> The Lord wrote on these tablets what he had written before, the Ten Commandments he had proclaimed to you on the mountain, out of the fire, on the day of the assembly. And the Lord gave them to me. **Deuteronomy 10:4 (NIV)**

> In the beginning was the Word, and the Word was with God, and the Word was God...The Word became flesh and made his dwelling among us. We have seen his glory, the glory of the one and only Son, who came from the Father, full of grace and truth. **John 1:1/14 (NIV)**

In turn, our response and all of our commitments to God also begin with words.

> Because all the people hung on his words. **Luke 19:48 (NIV)**

> Take words with you and return to the Lord. Say to him: "Forgive all our sins and receive us graciously, that we may offer the fruit of our lips. Assyria cannot save us; we will not mount warhorses. We will never again say 'Our gods' to what our own hands have made, for in you the fatherless find compassion." **Hosea 14:2-3 (NIV)**

> For it is with your heart that you believe and are justified, and it is with your mouth that you profess your faith and are saved. **Romans 10:10 (NIV)**

Have you ever wondered why the people in the Bible went through elaborate processes of speaking words whether it was in the confession of their sins, affirmation of their commitment, celebration of God in praise, supplication for help or lamentation over troubles? Why was it never enough to simply make up their minds in their thoughts rather than broadcast it, since God knows the thoughts of our hearts? Because words contain a force that causes movement in the heart of the speaker and hearers, as well as in the forces that control the universe.

In the story of Jacob, the Angel who wrestled with him could not prevail over him until he brought him to a place of dependence by dislocating his thigh bone. As a result, Jacob was forced to lean on the man and as he came into this position of vulnerability, where he could not continue in his own willfulness, he asked for God's help

– bless me. Then God asked him a question that allowed Jacob to say what God already knew but needed Jacob to fully acknowledge. God was telling Jacob that He could not be blessed as long as he was a trickster. But Jacob had to first confess with his own lips who he was.

> Then the man said, "Let me go, for it is daybreak." But Jacob replied, "I will not let you go unless you bless me." The man asked him, "What is your name?" "Jacob," he answered. Then the man said, "Your name will no longer be Jacob, but Israel, because you have struggled with God and with humans and have over-come." **Genesis 32:26-28 (NIV)**

This was so important in the transformative encounter that Jacob had by this riverside, because people can become so accustomed to something bad that its actual nature eludes them. We become desensitized to the full impact of words, actions and beliefs because we experience them constantly. This is how our generation has lost its empathy; through the constant barrage of violent images flooding our consciousness from the television and internet. To bring us back to where our conscience is reawakened to the horrors of what we have accepted as normal, God shows us the nature and extent of our errors. Realization of our sin creates remorse and remorse requires admission of guilt. Just as in our court systems, when a person enters a guilty plea, they must say it to the hearing of the court. In God's presence, we do not just accept our guilt; we go forward to vocalize it to His and our own hearing, saying 'I have been guilty of doing such-and-such. With this action we start to come to full self-realization.

The Spiritual Principle of Confession

Why is so important to audibly confess our sins to God? It is essential because our words multiply the force of our thoughts and bring them back into our consciousness with fresh power. Speaking words to ourselves multiply the impact of the words. It is more powerful to speak words than to merely think them. That is why words can be hard to speak sometimes. That is why some men find it hard to say 'I love you' and many women would rather say 'He slept with me' than 'I slept with him.' Those words carry with them an impact that we want to avoid.

Because affirmative words dry up in a relationship, the embers of its love grow cold and the couple grows apart. If the persons in marriage only speak to each other about the bills, the children, their community, relatives and their jobs, the relationship soon loses the vital emotional contents which connected the two persons in the first place. Words stoke a fire in our souls and whatever we say contains a potent force that conveys a dimension of reality that is difficult for our spirits to ignore. Words force something to fully occupy our spirits.

This is the reason people usually find it hard to admit to themselves the wrong things that they have been doing. The reason we live in denial at all is because the impact of acknowledging the reality is almost impossible to ignore. Even when people do that wrong thing intentionally, they will still find ways to avoid directly acknowledging the fact. It is hard for anyone to say to themselves 'I am lazy,' 'I am a thief.' 'I am an irresponsible father,' I am an immoral woman,' 'I am a dishonest employee,' 'I am a hypocrite,' or 'I am an abusive person.'

Even in private, these words are hard to speak because the moment you begin to do that, the words come back to you with such force that you actually see yourself as you really are and have to do something about it. If what you acknowledged about yourself is something bad, you feel impelled to change your ways. And if it is something good, you feel propelled to live up to your words. Words contain a force in themselves that have the capability to move, to wound, to heal, to raise up and to cast down.

Words spur motion in our spirits that cause movement in our bodies and alter our behavior. And this is why prayers of confessions in the Bible are always accompanied with movement. When people confess their sins, they fall on the ground, strip off their fine clothes, cover themselves in sack-cloth, break down in tears and pour dust and ashes on their bodies. These actions are not just an outward act. They are the result of what happens when people actually see their sinfulness, not from the downplayed viewpoint of our minds but from the truthful insight imparted by God's spirit.

When any catastrophic event is brought with the full force of its impact into our spirit, there is always a physical response.

This was true for Jacob when he was told that his son, Joseph, was dead.

> He recognized it and said, "It is my son's robe! Some ferocious animal has devoured him. Joseph has surely been torn to pieces." Then Jacob tore his clothes, put on sackcloth and mourned for his son many days. **Genesis 37:33-34 (NIV)**

It was true for Rizpah, the Concubine of Saul, when her two sons were executed.

> But the king took Armoni and Mephibosheth, the two sons of Aiah's daughter Rizpah, whom she had borne to Saul, together with the five sons of Saul's daughter Merab, whom she had borne to Adriel son of Barzillai the Meholathite. He handed them over to the Gibeonites, who killed them and exposed their bodies on a hill before the Lord. All seven of them fell together; they were put to death during the first days of the harvest, just as the barley harvest was beginning. Rizpah daughter of Aiah took sackcloth and spread it out for herself on a rock. From the beginning of the harvest till the rain poured down from the heavens on the bodies, she did not let the birds touch them by day or the wild animals by night. **2 Samuel 21:8-10 (NIV)**

It was true for Job, when he learned of the death of his children and the loss of his wealth. It was also true when he repented before God.

> At this, Job got up and tore his robe and shaved his head. Then he fell to the ground in worship. **Job 1:20 (NIV)**

> Therefore I despise myself and repent in dust and ashes." **Job 42:6 (NIV)**

When something fully affects our emotions, it will cause a spontaneous response in our bodies. Our bodies respond to what our minds feel. In fact, it is sometimes a measure of how genuinely we feel the emotion. What the mind feels, it expresses as movements in our bodies. This is why sad or depressed people do not feel like raising their heads. Rather, they hunch their shoulders, bow their heads and slouch as they walk. In the same way the emotions and postures of joy, power and victory are unmistakable and almost universal.

It is for these reasons true repentance demands verbal confession and physical acts such as kneeling, prostration and weeping. In confessing our sins, we repeat our errors to our own hearing, reinforcing the sorrow that we feel about them and moving our bodies to respond appropriately to that sorrow. By doing this we allow ourselves to experience the full process of confronting our sins, grieving for our rebelliousness with heart felt sorrow and as a result fully appreciating the comfort of the Holy Spirit when He eventually ministers forgiveness and hope to us. Without going through this process in one form or another, repentance may be shallow and short lived.

The Importance of Confessing Our Sins

Below are the spiritual benefits of intentionally confessing our sins to God

We See Our True Selves

It reveals our true selves to us and allows us to experience the full weight of our sins, not from our selfish point of view, but from the point of view of a just God and the victims of our actions. Seeing ourselves through God's eyes helps us to change positions to a place where He can use us.

> And they were calling to one another: "Holy, holy, holy is the Lord Almighty; the whole earth is full of his glory." At the sound of their voices the doorposts and thresholds shook and the temple was filled with smoke. "Woe to me!" I cried. "I am ruined! For I am

a man of unclean lips, and I live among a people of unclean lips, and my eyes have seen the King, the Lord Almighty." **Isaiah 6:3-5 (NIV)**

It Creates Godly Sorrow

It opens up avenues for experiencing earnest grief which is necessary for repentance. Deep grief will result in a shift in how we perceive sin, from acceptable to abominable. This will create in us the power to forcefully reject the sin.

> Godly sorrow brings repentance that leads to salvation and leaves no regret, but worldly sorrow brings death. See what this godly sorrow has produced in you: what earnestness, what eagerness to clear yourselves, what indignation, what alarm, what longing, what concern, what readiness to see justice done. At every point you have proved yourselves to be innocent in this matter. **2 Corinthians 7:10-11 (NIV)**

We Receive Spiritual Cleansing

It cleanses us emotionally and spiritually. The experience of confession and repentance are cathartic in effect, the believer leaves the place of prayer feeling relieved because the burdens have been left in God's presence.

> If we confess our sins, he is faithful and just and will forgive us our sins and purify us from all unrighteousness. **1 John 1:9 (NIV)**

It Creates True Repentance

Repentance is not some feeling or shedding tears. Repentance is a change in our disposition that results in visible changes in the way we live. Repentance is to provide proof of your submission to God by a changed lifestyle.

> But when he saw many of the Pharisees and Sadducees coming to where he was baptizing, he said to them: "You brood of vipers! Who warned you to flee from the coming wrath? Produce fruit in keeping with repentance. And do not think you can say to yourselves, 'We have Abraham as our father.' I tell you that out of these stones God can raise up children for Abraham. The ax is already at the root of the trees, and every tree that does not produce good fruit will be cut down and thrown into the fire.
> **Matthew 3:7-10 (NIV)**

We Receive Forgiveness and Qualify For God's Grace

Confession opens doors of Grace for us because we have now come into agreement with God's judgments over our lives instead of resisting His sentence. To prosper in the verse below is not about money, but it means that the person will not be able to progress. But will always be held back by the judgment of God and the consequences of their actions.

> Whoever conceals their sins does not prosper, but the one who confesses and renounces them finds mercy. **Proverbs 28:13 (NIV)**

> When I kept silent, my bones wasted away through my groaning all day long. For day and night your

hand was heavy on me; my strength was sapped as in the heat of summer. Then I acknowledged my sin to you and did not cover up my iniquity. I said, "I will confess my transgressions to the Lord." And you forgave the guilt of my sin. **Psalm 32:3-5 (NIV)**

But if they will confess their sins and the sins of their ancestors—their unfaithfulness and their hostility toward me, which made me hostile toward them so that I sent them into the land of their enemies— then when their uncircumcised hearts are humbled and they pay for their sin, I will remember my covenant with Jacob and my covenant with Isaac and my covenant with Abraham, and I will remember the land. **Leviticus 26:40-42 (NIV)**

The Act of Confession

When we confess our sins and errors to God, we will find certain elements recurring in our prayers. These elements are also present in the confessional prayers of people in the Bible and are the natural steps that the Holy Spirit guides us through as we proceed from one spiritual level to a higher one.

Recognition

This is the heart of confession, which simply means to 'agree with' God in what He has said about us. Recognition is a confirmation of our submission.

> In all that has happened to us, you have remained righteous; you have acted faithfully, while we acted

wickedly. Our kings, our leaders, our priests and our ancestors did not follow your law; they did not pay attention to your commands or the statutes you warned them to keep. Even while they were in their kingdom, enjoying your great goodness to them in the spacious and fertile land you gave them, they did not serve you or turn from their evil ways. **Nehemiah 9:33-35 (NIV)**

Renunciation and Repentance

In renouncing our sins, we reject them. We repudiate our former claims of being right or helpless. Having rejected our previous position, we begin to progress toward changing our ways. Renunciation is verbal and internal. Repentance is action based.

> Let the wicked forsake their ways and the unrighteous their thoughts. Let them turn to the Lord, and he will have mercy on them, and to our God, for he will freely pardon. **Isaiah 55:7 (NIV)**

Renewal

We find assurance of peace and blessedness in the presence of God. And the burden of guilt is lifted from our hearts. Our prayer of repentance is replaced with thanksgiving and praise. God's healing process begins inside us.

> Repent, then, and turn to God, so that your sins may be wiped out, that times of refreshing may come from the Lord, **Acts 3:19 (NIV)**

Reaffirmation

We hold on to God's word declaring us free from sin and keep declaring ourselves liberated. We refuse to take feelings of guilt as evidence of God's judgment but continue to affirm His word to us.

> If our hearts condemn us, we know that God is greater than our hearts, and He knows everything.
> **1 John 3:20 (NIV)**

The Marks of Repentance

The real evidence of submission to God is shown when we leave the place of prayer. Our prayers of confession and repentance are a private agreement with God. It is our promise of commitment to His Word – an oath to be faithful.

When we leave that place of prayer, we actually begin to live up to the commitments that we made in God's presence. If we follow our declaration with actions, the result is that we will appear different to others.

> By their fruit you will recognize them. Do people pick grapes from thorn bushes, or figs from thistles? Likewise, every good tree bears good fruit, but a bad tree bears bad fruit. A good tree cannot bear bad fruit, and a bad tree cannot bear good fruit. **Matthew 7:16-18 (NIV)**

Repentance is shown in practical action, in affects behavior. The Bible uses the word 'conversion' to describe what happens when a person repents. They experience a level of internal reconstruction that leaves them visibly transformed. That change is so pervasive it touches every facet of their lives and it is virtually impossible for the individual to hide their new identity.

Repentance is a change of values that is totally invasive and leaves no part of our hearts untouched. We change our way of thinking. We change our direction and highest purposes. We change the things that we hold as our highest treasure – our God. We change in our self-perception. Repentance impacts on us to the point where it is reflected in:

The People We Respect

Because of our views of money, sin and righteousness change, we also begin to evaluate people based on how they match our new way of thinking. You cannot repent and have the same old heroes, friends and mentors.

> The fearful heart will know and understand, and the stammering tongue will be fluent and clear. No longer will the fool be called noble nor the scoundrel be highly respected. For fools speak folly, their hearts are bent on evil: They practice ungodliness and spread error concerning the Lord; the hungry they leave empty and from the thirsty they withhold water. **Isaiah 32:4-6 (NIV)**

The Way We View Money

True repentance will begin to bring us to the place where we value people more than things and as such become more willing to part with our property to help people.

Confession and Repentance

> Whoever claims to love God yet hates a brother or sister is a liar. For whoever does not love their brother and sister, whom they have seen, cannot love God, whom they have not seen. **1 John 4:20 (NIV)**

> "Is not this the kind of fasting I have chosen: to loose the chains of injustice and untie the cords of the yoke, to set the oppressed free and break every yoke? Is it not to share your food with the hungry and to provide the poor wanderer with shelter - when you see the naked, to clothe them, and not to turn away from your own flesh and blood? **Isaiah 58: 6-7 (NIV)**

The Way We Use Power

We practice more equity and show a higher degree of fairness to those weaker than we are. These may be our subordinates, employees or the poor.

> Why have we fasted,' they say, 'and you have not seen it? Why have we humbled ourselves, and you have not noticed?' "Yet on the day of your fasting, you do as you please and exploit all your workers. Your fasting ends in quarreling and strife, and in striking each other with wicked fists. You cannot fast as you do today and expect your voice to be heard on high. **Isaiah 58: 3-4 (NIV)**

CHAPTER FOUR
INNER HEALING AND DELIVERANCE – PART 1

There is something beyond what we see and feel at work in the lives of people. We all like to believe that our thoughts, decisions and actions are our own, and that there is nothing and no one imposing them on us. But the truth is there is more; just as the government makes laws that control our behavior, there are powers that influence the outcome of our lives. The reason we cannot see this is because even before we got to the age where we could make conscious choices, that power has been at work in our lives to determine the makeup of our minds and environments. With the result that when we eventually start to choose, we do so from the limited options of what has already been predetermined for us.

This is one reason many young people can resolve at an early age to be as different from their parents as possible. But by the time they get to their middle age, many of them realize that they have become more like their parents than they care to admit. This is in spite of doing their best to discard physical gestures, habits of speech, choice of clothes and even diets that reminded them of their parent. Instead of becoming different, they find that as they get older, they respond to life's challenges exactly as their parents did. As a result of this, their finances, relationships and spiritual lives end up closely resembling those of their parents.

The reason this happens is that these young people never understood the roots of the situation they were trying to avoid. They merely attacked the surface (outward effects) of the problem and not its roots (internal causes). They could not see that there is a process at work inside each of us which frames our behavior and causes us to draw to ourselves the very things we fear. This is why changing a person's physical location, does not guarantee a change in their circumstances; they would just continue living as they had always done in the new place. This was true of Israel in the wilderness; they had been crying for freedom from slavery but when they were freed, they began to clamor to be returned to the old environment.

> During that long period, the king of Egypt died. The Israelites groaned in their slavery and cried out, and their cry for help because of their slavery went up to God. God heard their groaning and he remembered his covenant with Abraham, with Isaac and with Jacob. So God looked on the Israelites and was concerned about them. **Exodus 2:23-25 (NIV)**

> Now the length of time the Israelite people lived in Egypt was 430 years. At the end of the 430 years, to the very day, all the Lord's divisions left Egypt. Because the Lord kept vigil that night to bring them out of Egypt, on this night all the Israelites are to keep vigil to honor the Lord for the generations to come. **Exodus 12:40-42 (NIV)**

> Why is the Lord bringing us to this land only to let us fall by the sword? Our wives and children will be taken as plunder. Wouldn't it be better for us to go back to Egypt?" And they said to each other,

> "We should choose a leader and go back to Egypt."
> **Numbers 14:3-4 (NIV)**

The slave mindset that they had inside them could only function within an environment of bondage. Freedom ran counter to their psychological predisposition; its demands for responsibility, self-regulation, and purposeful living were just too much to for them to handle. They wanted to return to that place where their customary patterns of thought and behavior were acceptable. This is exactly how people continue to repeat the ideas, choices, errors and results of their past because those things have been hardwired into their souls by a superior spiritual power. For Israel that power could be visibly identified as Pharaoh, but for us, it will require introspection, prayer, discernment and spiritual insight to recognize the forces at work in our lives.

Understanding Generational Curses

The Case of Simeon and Levi

In the thirty-fourth chapter of the book of Genesis, we find a sad story. Jacob, having escaped his brother Esau, by the help of God, had settled his family in lands belonging to the Canaanite city of Shechem. Sometime after his arrival, his teenage daughter, Dinah, went to visit with her Canaanite girlfriends in the city, when the Crown-Prince of the City State seized her forcefully and raped her. Afterwards, he sent his Father, the King of Shechem, to speak with Jacob, expressing his desire to marry his daughter.

> When Jacob heard that his daughter Dinah had been defiled, his sons were in the fields with his livestock; so he did nothing about it until they came

> home. Then Shechem's father Hamor went out to talk with Jacob. Meanwhile, Jacob's sons had come in from the fields as soon as they heard what had happened. They were shocked and furious, because Shechem had done an outrageous thing in Israel by sleeping with Jacob's daughter—a thing that should not be done. **Genesis 34:5-7 (NIV)**

Of course, Jacob was enraged. First, the man had insulted his family name by violating his daughter. Secondly, his family did not intermarry with the people of Canaan – which was probably why the Canaanite Prince forced himself on the girl, to put her father in a difficult position. However, he did not give them an answer; he waited until his sons returned. After deliberating amongst themselves, Jacob's sons gave the King their terms; that they would only intermarry with them if all the men of that city became circumcised like they were.

Convinced by the Prince, all the men of Shechem were circumcised. But the sons of Jacob had only demanded this from the city in order to eliminate their military advantage. On the third day after these men had been circumcised, when their pain was intense, Simeon and Levi went into the city with swords and murdered all men in it, including the King and the Prince. Afterwards, the rest of their brothers came and looted the city, taking and selling their women and children off as slaves, no doubt raping many of them in the process. Naturally, when Jacob heard it, he was livid and had to hurriedly leave the area.

> Three days later, while all of them were still in pain, two of Jacob's sons, Simeon and Levi, Dinah's brothers, took their swords and attacked the unsuspecting city, killing every male. They put Hamor and his

son, Shechem to the sword and took Dinah from Shechem's house and left. The sons of Jacob came upon the dead bodies and looted the city where their sister had been defiled. They seized their flocks and herds and donkeys and everything else of theirs in the city and out in the fields. They carried off all their wealth and all their women and children, taking as plunder everything in the houses. Then Jacob said to Simeon and Levi, "You have brought trouble on me by making me obnoxious to the Canaanites and Perizzites, the people living in this land. We are few in number, and if they join forces against me and attack me, I and my household will be destroyed." But they replied, "Should he have treated our sister like a prostitute?" **Genesis 34:25-31**

The story did not end there, at least not for Jacob; he kept it well in mind as we shall see later. But there are interesting parallels in the past behavior of Jacob and the actions of his sons.

- First, there is a regard for fatherly authority. Just like Jacob had disregarded his father to get the blessing, Simeon and Levi also overlooked Jacob to destroy Shechem.

- Just as Jacob whose principal tool had been deceit, these two practiced an even higher level of deceit. They were so twisted that even Jacob was shocked.

- Simeon and Levi did not submit to God in the pursuit of justice and truth but resorted to violence. Similarly, Jacob had not waited for God to resolve the issue of his father's refusal to bless him.

We see the ways of Jacob, replicated and amplified in the lives of his sons. But we have to ask how this influence could continue in his family after Jacob's surrender to God. Jacob had submitted but his sons had not. At this point, these sons of Jacob sons were already grown and set in their ways. They took after their father's past behavior and not his current lifestyle. Jacob's encounter had been private and personal, there was no way he could assign its benefits to his sons, and they had to experience it for themselves. This is possibly why God kept Abraham from having sons until he had come to a place of proper understanding of God and relationship with Him. This would ensure that Isaac would grow up under the new spiritual atmosphere of his father's life and not have a backlog to deal with. Unfortunately, the case was different for Jacob's children; their conduct took him back to the past.

Decades later, when it came time for Jacob to make the fatherly pronouncements that would usher his sons into their destinies, Jacob spoke over Simeon and Levi with words that resembled a curse more than a blessing. And he did this on the basis of their actions at Shechem. Jacob's words not only set a limit on the successes Simeon and Levi experienced, it also set a cap on the extent of power and they posterity would enjoy.

> Simeon and Levi are brothers - their swords are weapons of violence. Let me not enter their council, let me not join their assembly, for they have killed men in their anger and hamstrung oxen as they pleased. Cursed be their anger, so fierce, and their fury, so cruel! I will scatter them in Jacob and disperse them in Israel. **Genesis 49:5-7 (NIV)**

This meant that the generations of Simeon and Levi would have limited power. Because whether it is in politics, business or war, the size of one's electorate, market or army confers real power. By scattering them, he is saying that even if they have many men, they would be incapable of collective action and thereby mustering the full impact of their power. They could not translate their population into influence because there would be no cohesion between their forces. Rather, they would remain under the domination of those who although weaker or fewer were capable of unified action. These descendants of Simeon and Levi would enter the Promised Land but could never rise to prominence.

Should Jacob have cursed his sons? Did he actually curse these men? Is it even possible for one man to curse another? The pronouncements of authority figures over a person depend on the individual's actions for power. Blessing, as well as cursing, must link up with personal character to take effect. Thus, as Jacob looked over the lives of his grandsons with the perceptiveness and foresight parents have when they observe their children, he could see their future based on their present. He noted their constant resort to deceit and violence and how these traits would prevent them from finding stability. It would impair their ability to form alliances in business, politics and war. They would always remain small because they could not be trusted. Jacob did not curse his children; but before we go forward to that, we must understand the mechanics that operate behind curses.

The Origin of Curses

All curses come through the violation of God's law and our twisted personal beliefs. Curses need power to take effect and they draw that power from two sources. A curse can draw its power from our own wrong actions. It can also draw power from our beliefs.

When negative words or curses are pronounced against us, they cannot take hold unless we invest power in them by believing the words. In other words, we accept that this person has authority over our lives and that what they say about us matters. Otherwise, those words are powerless to hurt us. This means that a curse lies within the power of the individual and cannot operate until we give it legitimacy. That legitimacy is conferred through wrong conduct and beliefs.

The first curse mentioned in the Bible was against Adam and Eve, which was in reality a declaration of the inevitable consequences that would now attend their work, relationships, happiness and future as a result of their choices. God was telling them that based upon their electing to transfer their allegiance to Satan, their lives under the domination of darkness would have these results. He said it all happened because of them; because the means to be-the-cause-of.

> To the woman he said, "I will make your pains in childbearing very severe; with painful labor you will give birth to children. Your desire will be for your husband, and he will rule over you." To Adam he said, "Because you listened to your wife and ate fruit from the tree about which I commanded you, 'You must not eat from it,' "Cursed is the ground because of you; through painful toil you will eat food from it all the days of your life. It will produce thorns and thistles for you, and you will eat the plants of the field. By the sweat of your brow you will eat your food until you return to the ground, since from it you were taken; for dust you are and to dust you will return." **Genesis 3:16-19 (NIV)**

This is illustrated in the second curse of the Bible, the curse against Cain. Here, God makes it clear that the curse would come from the earth, which Cain had violated when he killed his brother Abel. And to demonstrate that the role of God is mercy, when Cain complained about the weight of his punishment, God gave him some reprieve.

> Now you are under a curse and driven from the ground, which opened its mouth to receive your brother's blood from your hand. When you work the ground, it will no longer yield its crops for you. You will be a restless wanderer on the earth." Cain said to the Lord, "My punishment is more than I can bear. Today you are driving me from the land, and I will be hidden from your presence; I will be a restless wanderer on the earth, and whoever finds me will kill me." But the Lord said to him, "Not so; anyone who kills Cain will suffer vengeance seven times over." Then the Lord put a mark on Cain so that no one who found him would kill him. **Genesis 4:11-15 (NIV)**

The implication of this is that curses are the results of human disobedience, and not God's vindictiveness. As previously noted, every human life is lived under the domination of a spiritual entity. If we uproot ourselves from God's house of freedom and migrate to Satan's camp of slavery, our lives will mirror that choice. We either advance the purpose of light or support the goals of darkness. When we disobey God, we indirectly empower Satan; there are no neutral territories. To not build something has the same effect as breaking it down after it is built.

> Whoever is not with me is against me, and whoever does not gather with me scatters. **Luke 11:23 (NIV)**

> One who is slack in his work is brother to one who destroys. **Proverbs 18:9 (NIV)**

We are cursed by our wrong words, beliefs, choices and actions. Even if Jacob had cursed his sons, that judgment would not have stood because there would be no basis for it. There would be nothing in the lives of the men to justify the curse; no door by which Satan could come in. Any spirit attempting to bring them under the curse would find no legal hold; misconduct by which it could move their lives in the direction of the curse.

> Like a fluttering sparrow or a darting swallow, an undeserved curse does not come to rest. **Proverbs 26:2 (NIV)**

> God is not a human being, and he will not lie. He is not a human, and he does not change his mind. What he says he will do, he does [will he not do it?]. What he promises, he makes come true [will he not fulfill it/make it come true?]. He told [commanded] me to bless them, so I cannot change the blessing. He has found [observes] no wrong in the people of Jacob; he saw no fault [trouble] in Israel. The Lord their God is with them, and they praise their King.
> **Numbers 23:19-21 (EXB)**

Curses result when we leave the place God has assigned for us. By breaking out of these limits, we step beyond the barriers erected for our protection. As a result, we fall prey to evil forces which take us captive and destroy our tranquility.

> Anyone who digs a pit might fall into it; anyone who knocks down [breeches] a wall might be bitten by a snake; **Ecclesiastes 10:8 (EXB)**

> A person who leaves [wanders from] his home is like a bird that leaves [wanders from] its nest. **Proverbs 27:8 (EXB)**

The words that Jacob spoke to his sons were not curses but the results that they had determined for themselves by their choices to obey or disobey what he taught them. He was allocating them their rewards – in the Promised Land - based on their works – in their present state.

> Then Jacob called for his sons and said: "Gather around so I can tell you what will happen to you in days to come. **Genesis 49:1 (NIV)**

> All these are the twelve tribes of Israel, and this is what their father said to them when he blessed them, giving each the blessing appropriate to him. **Genesis 49:28 (NIV)**

In reality, he blessed them, since he did not deny any of them entry into the Promised Land. But he did mean that although they would be blessed, they would never receive its fullness due to their lack of character. He was telling Simeon and Levi, that this was what they deserved based on what they had done. They purchased failure, pain, bitterness and limitation by trading in violence and deceit. But if this is the case, why extend the results to their children? Because of the operations of the spiritual principles of blessing and cursing; the children inherited the fate of their fathers not through the decisions of Jacob but the actions of Simeon and Levi. The fathers would set the children's feet on the same path as they had walked, condemning them to the same results.

The Operation of Curses

Every curse begins life as human misconduct but becomes a spiritual force that multiplies in impact over time. The curse operating in the lives of Simeon and Levi took origin from their rebellion, deception, violence and murder. The power of a curse first enters through sin and then consolidates its hold as that original sin is repeated continuously. The spirit entering the person's life reengineers it so completely that they become owned by the sin. It becomes their habitual way of life and this entrenches the hold of the entity on their minds and also guarantees it a place in their future.

As the person begins to have children, that satanic spirit also seeks to expand its control to include the children. That governing entity over the lives of the parents works to create circumstances that force the child into patterns of behavior conducive to the prolongation of its domination of the family. This ensures that the child inherits the father's mindsets and becomes an heir to his results, namely, the curse. There are many instruments the Devil employs to achieve this goal but the primary one is the parents themselves. Parents create a way of thinking, a pattern of behaving and a home atmosphere that predisposes the child to certain habits. Parent's choices also open doors to people and experiences that wound the child's spirit.

A child may suffer repeated nightmares, which are in reality attacks upon the young soul, as evil spirits which the parents have given permission to operate in the home assaults the child's consciousness. These nightmares could create fear, terror, hate or lust in the child, depending on the identity of the spirit behind it. The impact of such experiences is that even in their waking hours, the child carries that emotion until it dominates their whole life. As they become teenagers, these stored up thoughts and feelings begin to manifest in specific behaviors. Often the parent does not know that this is happening and even if they did, they would be powerless to stop it.

Children could also be abused by people, who have been allowed to enter their lives because parents were not spiritually sensitive; created a home atmosphere that drove the child to that person or they were absent. This is how a lot of young people – male and female - get raped. This destroys their psyche and alters how they view themselves sexually. Becoming sexualized, they lose the power to control themselves, do not value their bodies and are unable to define what proper sexual relations are. This is the origin of prostitution, lesbianism and homosexuality for many people.

Another example is when the child lives in a dysfunctional home environment and observes the abusive behaviors of their parents and other people allowed into the child's space. On a deeper level, the child hates the life and desperately wants to escape it. However, they go forward and discover that the exact same things that happened in their parents' lives are happening to them. They attract the same kinds of relationships and encounter the same kind of situations. The reason is that although they hate that life, it is all they know and their default mode of behavior. They are trying to act different but have never seen or experienced differently. They are following a script written for them.

All in all, a generational spirit works behind the scenes to navigate the individual's life into the path of people and experiences that bend them into repeating specific patterns through their lifetime. By manipulating their physical, emotional and mental environments, the springs of a person's life, their destinies are fixed. It is amazing how people can leave their city or country to another, and in the new location manage to end up with the exact same kinds of people as they left behind in the old place. With a net result that it feels as if they never left. Or how do some people repeat the same relationship patterns over and over again? With each new man or woman, they tell themselves that it is going to be different this time. Yet in the end, the relationship turns out exactly like the previous ones, different only in the personal details of this new person.

In trying to explain their lives, some people will say things like 'I have no luck,' 'I never meet good men (or women),' 'I am accident or trouble-prone.' And they are right! They have identified that they have an inexplicable tendency of attracting certain kinds of things and people into their lives. They may want to act different but cannot; they see the course their life is taking and sense its inevitable outcome but cannot escape it. Some have an unshakeable fear that they will end up like their parents; because they realize that they are in the grip of whatever destroyed their parents. Their lives are running on invisible tracks and they operate under a fixed ceiling. They are in the hold of something that keeps them in their familiar places, what the bible refers to as a Familiar Spirit. The word Familiar is from the Latin familiaris that is, family. Familiar spirit = family spirit.

It is for these reasons that Jacob could tell Simeon and Levi that their personal lack of character would serve as a spiritual ceiling limiting their children for hundreds of years to come. Their personal faults would give access to a spirit that would create an ancestral curse. These men already had sons who were grown up and Jacob could see the same character traits present in the children of Simeon and Levi. He noted how the thinking, beliefs, expectations, actions and relationships of his own sons fixed the attitudes and fates of his grandchildren. This is why the Bible says that the children of the wicked go astray from birth. They begin to get twisted before they are even born, because from the womb they are bombarded with the negative words and wicked spirits of their fathers.

> Their deeds do not permit them to return to their God. A spirit of prostitution is in their heart; they do not acknowledge the Lord. **Hosea 5:4 (NIV)**
>
> For forty years I was angry with that generation; I said, 'They are a people whose hearts go astray, and they have not known my ways.' **Psalm 95:10 (NIV)**
>
> Even from birth the wicked go astray; from the womb they are wayward, spreading lies. **Psalm 58:3 (NIV)**

What has become clear is that there are two dimensions to the operation of the curse in a person's life. There is the character aspect which has to do with the person's beliefs, thoughts and actions; mindset characteristics and corresponding lifestyles that flow from them. These serve as doorways and anchors to give unreserved access and control over the person to a spiritual force. Then, there is the demonic aspect; a spirit working behind the scenes to predispose the person to continue to act in a certain way. This spirit hounds the person's life creating fortuitous events that play into its goal of destroying the individual. The mindset and lifestyles of the person is the spirit's operational license and its legal right is to oppress them. The demonic aspect is the jailer that keeps the person in prison.

Escape From Bondage

Is there even a way out? Is there any hope of escape? Thankfully, the answer is yes. And just as personal choices and actions were the origins of the curse, personal choices and actions also kick-start our deliverance. It is important to note that merely being in church or even being active in church work will not bring us deliverance. We can be in church and labor under a curse. The actions that will set us on the road to freedom originate at the level of internal change and not religious devotion. The sons of Jacob were heirs of God's promise to Abraham, yet that spiritual heritage did not overshadow their individual outcomes. As a matter of fact, they could live in the land of blessedness and experience trouble. In the same way, people can be in the house of God and everyone around them gets blessed while they live in darkness.

It is possible to be free because the descendants of one of these two men, Simeon and Levi, did break free. Four hundred years after the pronouncement of those words by Jacob, the sons of Simeon and Levi were presented with an opportunity to escape their spiritual limitations. It was a chance to disrupt the cycle of events in their lives by breaking with their past behavior and crafting a new direction for their lives. By taking this opportunity, they would step out of their old mindsets and in return, reap a harvest of new consequences and a different life. Sadly, only the descendants of one man took action, Levi.

> So he stood at the entrance to the camp and said, "Whoever is for the Lord, come to me." And all the Levites rallied to him. Then he said to them, "This is what the Lord, the God of Israel, says: 'Each man strap a sword to his side. Go back and forth through the camp from one end to the other, each killing his brother and friend and neighbor.'" The Levites did as Moses commanded, and that day about three thousand of the people died. Then Moses said, "You have been set apart to the Lord today, for you were against your own sons and brothers, and he has blessed you this day." **Exodus 32:26-29 (NIV)**

If we look away from the gruesome details of this story, a few important lessons emerge.

- Levi had dedicated the same weapon and behavior that had gotten him into trouble to God. What was previously the instrument of his self will now became the emblem of his submission.

- He ceased to act for self. In the past, they had not acted with consideration for the safety and wellbeing of Israel. Now they acted to protect the nation.

- They submitted to the authority of Moses, unlike in the past when they had rebelled against the authority of their father, Jacob.

In effect, Levi did everything different from what they had done previously and got a blessing for it. Moses told them that because of their submission, God had blessed them – God was now going to set them apart. The curse of being scattered all over Israel now became the blessing of being dispatched across the nation as guardians of God's law. There was a reversal of the curse.

There are vital elements in this story that reveal to us the pathway to freedom from bondage to an ancestral curse.

Obedience

Everyone gets a chance every day to act differently and begin to make their way out of slavery. But most people never take it because changing requires a certain degree of dying, which might even mean alienation from people you love. Remember, that these old patterns of behavior have become entrenched and as a result, acting contrary to them can be a real struggle. It was that way for the sons of Levi. They were being asked to act against their own natural inclination and kill family members who had worshipped idols. To obey could not have been easy; it would have been comparable to losing a part of one's self. But it was a question of whom they loved more; themselves, their families or God. Freedom always hinges on obedience to God and that obedience has to be demonstrated.

Legitimate Authority

Legitimate authority acts as a hedge against destruction and as a conduit for blessings. The blessing is always conferred by a higher authority because blessedness means to be lifted up to a higher level than we currently experience. The highest authority is God but God uses men and women as instruments. He sends people into our lives, both to bring His blessing to us and also defend us against satanic forces. The first legitimate authorities in our lives are parents. Another level of legitimate authority is people set and sent into our lives as agents of God to bring about God's will in our lives. Submission to legitimate authority brings us under a canopy where God can act on our behalf.

> And without doubt the lesser is blessed by the greater. **Hebrews 7:7 (NIV)**

> Then he showed me Joshua the high priest standing before the angel of the Lord, and Satan standing at his right side to accuse him. The Lord said to Satan, "The Lord rebuke you, Satan! The Lord, who has chosen Jerusalem, rebuke you! Is not this man a burning stick snatched from the fire?" Now Joshua was dressed in filthy clothes as he stood before the angel. The angel said to those who were standing before him, "Take off his filthy clothes." Then he said to Joshua, "See, I have taken away your sin, and I will put fine garments on you." Then I said, "Put a clean turban on his head." So they put a clean turban on his head and clothed him, while the angel of the Lord stood by. **Zechariah 3:1-5 (NIV)**

The High Priest in the above verse was unaware of the spiritual struggle that was going on in his life. It was the prophet who spoke on his behalf and ensured that he got the glory reserved for him. In the same way, there are people who God sets in our lives to speak over our lives and break Satan's power. The hold of the curse is based on authority and requires a higher authority than we have to break out of. Hence it was Moses, who declared a change in the destiny of the sons of Levi. This is why it is important to honor the godly people sent into our lives, they stand as hedges.

> When a strong man, fully armed, guards his own house, his possessions are safe. But when someone stronger attacks and overpowers him, he takes away the armor in which the man trusted and divides up his plunder. **Luke 11:21-22 (NIV)**

Understanding the need for Deliverance

The level of power and authority required to break free from satanic oppression is often beyond the capability of the person under a curse. This is because their minds are often veiled by the power of Satan so that they cannot have spiritual insights. Additionally, their spirits are weakened to the point that they are unable to muster any significant resistance to the devilish power. This is why churches and ministries that understand spiritual warfare and satanic operations are necessary for obtaining complete freedom from a curse. They possess insight and discernment to detect and understand the spiritual forces at work in our lives and are also equipped with an anointing to break the satanic hold. The devil never willingly releases his captives; therefore freedom requires force and truth. The truth is the word of God that we have begun to obey. The force is the power of the Holy Spirit operating through the spiritual authority to release us from bondage.

> Can plunder be taken from warriors, or captives be rescued from the fierce? But this is what the Lord says: "Yes, captives will be taken from warriors, and plunder retrieved from the fierce; I will contend with those who contend with you, and your children I will save. I will make your oppressors eat their own flesh; they will be drunk on their own blood, as with

wine. Then all mankind will know that I, the Lord, am your Savior, your Redeemer, the Mighty One of Jacob." **Isaiah 49:24-26 (NIV)**

There are steps necessary for a person seeking deliverance.

Recognizing The Door

Specific counterfeit spirits operate through specific sins. Through the operation of the gifts of the spirit and by looking at the dominant thought patterns, habits and results of the person's life, the demonic influence can be identified. By identifying the spirit at work and the curse in operation, half of the battle is won.

> Then Joshua tore his clothes and fell facedown to the ground before the ark of the Lord, remaining there till evening. The elders of Israel did the same, and sprinkled dust on their heads. And Joshua said, "Alas, Sovereign Lord, why did you ever bring this person across the Jordan to deliver us into the hands of the Amorites to destroy us? If only we had been content to stay on the other side of the Jordan! Pardon your servant, Lord. What can I say, now that Israel has been routed by its enemies? ... The Lord said to Joshua, "Stand up! What are you doing down on your face? Israel has sinned; they have violated my covenant, which I commanded them to keep. They have taken some of the devoted things; they have stolen, they have lied, they have put them with their own possessions. **Joshua 7:6-11 (NIV)**

Renunciation

The person seeking deliverance must verbally and sincerely reject all connections to the spirit. Affirming that they do not belong to the entity and that it no longer has a claim in them because they have been not only submitted to God but have repented of their old ways.

> Then you will desecrate your idols overlaid with silver and your images covered with gold; you will throw them away like a menstrual cloth and say to them, "Away with you!" He will also send you rain for the seed you sow in the ground, and the food that comes from the land will be rich and plentiful. In that day your cattle will graze in broad meadows.
> **Isaiah 30:22-23 (NIV)**

Deliverance

The person seeking deliverance must submit themselves for prayers of deliverance, which will often include times of fasting. During this time, the minister conducting the deliverance takes authority over the evil spirit and casts it out of the person's life. This is a process of spiritual warfare and the conflicts might even break out into the physical realm in the form of illness, antagonistic behavior from people, attack on finances, and nightmares. But all these are the results of a desperate spirit attempting to intimidate the person into giving up. The only way to handle these incidents is to hold on to the Word of God, refuse to be drawn into sin and follow through on the process.

> But on Mount Zion will be deliverance; it will be holy, and Jacob will possess his inheritance. **Obadiah 17 (NIV)**

> And it shall come to pass in that day, that his burden shall be taken away from off thy shoulder, and his yoke from off thy neck, and the yoke shall be destroyed because of the anointing. **Isaiah 10:27 (AKJV)**

Fellowship With The Holy Spirit

After the hold of the Devil is broken, it is important for the person to become filled with the Holy Spirit and advance in their relationship with God by steadily allowing Him to lead them into living differently from how they used to live. It is necessary to move forward, bearing in mind that there is no static positions in the realm of the spirit, we are either going up or going down.

> Since, then, you have been raised with Christ, set your hearts on things above, where Christ is, seated at the right hand of God. Set your minds on things above, not on earthly things. For you died, and your life is now hidden with Christ in God. When Christ, who is your life, appears, then you also will appear with him in glory. Put to death, therefore, whatever belongs to your earthly nature: sexual immorality, impurity, lust, evil desires and greed, which is idolatry. Because of these, the wrath of God is coming. You used to walk in these ways, in the life you once lived. But now you must also rid yourselves of all such things as these: anger, rage, malice, slander, and filthy language from your lips. Do not lie to each other, since you have taken off your old self with its practices and have put on the new self, which is being renewed in knowledge in the image of its Creator. **Colossians 3:1-10 (NIV)**

For if you possess these qualities in increasing measure, they will keep you from being ineffective and unproductive in your knowledge of our Lord Jesus Christ. But whoever does not have them is nearsighted and blind, forgetting that they have been cleansed from their past sins. Therefore, my brothers and sisters, make every effort to confirm your calling and election. For if you do these things, you will never stumble, and you will receive a rich welcome into the eternal kingdom of our Lord and Savior Jesus Christ. **2 Peter 1:8-11 (NIV)**

CHAPTER FIVE

INNER HEALING AND DELIVERANCE – PART 2

There are spiritual entities that control or seek to control the world. If we look at a map of the physical world, we see geographical boundaries marking political territories. There is also a spiritual map of the world demarcated into territories that are under the control of specific evil spirits. These territories comprise of nations, cultures, cities, and families. And just as the citizens of political nations are distinguished by their language and law, the citizens of spiritual nations are distinct in the thoughts and notions that rule their lives.

This is why people from specific locations behave in specific ways. This is what we often attempt to try to explain when we say that people from such-and-such place behave in so-and-so way; they are known to be lazy, proud, greedy, cunning, violent, quick-tempered, dishonest, immoral, unfaithful in marriage, etc. We may also identify families with specific problems, like insanity, untimely death, absent fathers, prostitution, childlessness, incest, divorce, business failure, miscarriage, deformity, blindness, insanity, etc.

These spiritual entities are invisible governments and just like earthly governments, they have laws, demand obedience and service from their citizens and also offer benefits to them. These governments were represented by the idols most nations used to worship. And their laws included the rituals and customs by which these nations worshipped them. Some of these rituals contained lewd acts, perverted sex, human sacrifices, ritual prostitution, witchcraft and other kinds of acts which left their marks on the lives of the worshippers.

As a result of their subjection to these evil forces, the people inherited character traits associated with their worship and reaped repercussions in their lives. However, even when people migrated from worshipping idols, they could still manifest the results of living under the power of these entities, since they still lived under the character strongholds imposed by the evil spirit. As a matter of fact, these character strongholds were what kept people tied to those forces, not merely the act of worshipping those evil spirits.

Strongholds are recurrent negative thought patterns and lifestyles which destroy people. Yet the people persist in those actions either because they do not understand that it is the cause of their problems or they are in the grip of it and cannot break free. Strongholds are the means by which spirits hold and own people. The negative actions open doors to demonic spirits and the demonic spirits lead the person into worse negative behavior. Thus, people can become hopelessly bound.

> Although they claimed to be wise, they became fools and exchanged the glory of the immortal God for images made to look like a mortal human being and birds and animals and reptiles. Therefore God gave them over in the sinful desires of their hearts to sexual impurity for the degrading of their bodies with one another. They exchanged the truth about God for a lie, and worshiped and served created things rather than the Creator - who is forever

> praised. Amen. Because of this, God gave them over to shameful lusts. Even their women exchanged natural sexual relations for unnatural ones. In the same way the men also abandoned natural relations with women and were inflamed with lust for one another. Men committed shameful acts with other men, and received in themselves the due penalty for their error. Romans 1:22-32 (NIV)

This happens to people because even though they had changed their locations, they still lived under the influence of these old spirits. By retaining the mindsets of their ancestors, they also experienced their results. The above may also be true for individuals who, though their past generations did not worship idols, have knowingly or unknowingly opened doors to spirits, by participating in acts that attracted these demonic forces into their lives, such as perverted sex, bloodshed, drug use, involvement in occult practices and witchcraft (even for fun, through books online games and television).

The two elements that allow ancestral curses to remain in anyone's life are;

- Rebellion and
- Lack of character

Rebellion is the sin of not submitting to God's government over our lives. Lack of character is willful disrespect for what we clearly know to be true, right and just. Rebellion against God is automatically submission to Satan. Submission to Satan, gives him the legal right to harm. And to keep us perpetually enslaved, the Devil works rebellion and error into our spirit, so that he will always have a foothold in our lives. But when we realize and repent of our rebellion, God begins to work our deliverance from the Devil.

Transformation

Upon submitting our lives to God and pledging obedience to His word, we need to surrender ourselves for deliverance ministrations. Through submission to God we invalidate all covenants and agreements that connected us to that evil Spirit, making its continued operation in our lives illegal. Through deliverance, the Demonic spirit is addressed and sent out of our lives. The process of deliverance may require us to identify relationship connections, personal actions and words, other people's actions and words, or details of our personal and family histories that served as doorways of the spirits. Once these are identified, we must take action to neutralize their power.

- To facilitate and complete our deliverance, we have to do the following:
- Forgive and let go of hurt, bitterness and hate
- Repent of past actions that empowered Satan against us
- Restitution: actions such as calling up people we have wronged in the past and reconciling with them.
- Destroy all tokens of occultism and witchcraft in our lives
- Remove any thing that serves as a link between us and people that empower our past
- End relationships that reinforce our wrong behaviors

Inner Healing and Deliverance – Part 2

Deliverance is only the starting point of our journey of freedom from the hold of ancestral curses. From this point we must move forward and away from our past ways of thinking and acting. Progressively weakening our former self and growing stronger in the new person that we are becoming.

> As a result, they do not live the rest of their earthly lives for evil human desires, but rather for the will of God. For you have spent enough time in the past doing what pagans choose to do—living in debauchery, lust, drunkenness, orgies, carousing and detestable idolatry. They are surprised that you do not join them in their reckless, wild living, and they heap abuse on you. **1 Peter 4:2-4 (NIV)**

A New You

Bearing in mind that the root of the curse was not just the ancestral spirit but also our own lack of character, therefore the key to securing our freedom, after we have gone through deliverance, is to change more and more from the person that we used to be. As we have already noted, there are no neutral territories in the spirit realm. We cannot escape from the camp of Satan and not work towards becoming part of the family of God. If we attempt to do this what happens is that we unconsciously slip back into satanic bondage.

> "When an impure spirit comes out of a person, it goes through arid places seeking rest and does not find it. Then it says, 'I will return to the house I left.' When it arrives, it finds the house unoccupied, swept clean and put in order. Then it goes and takes with it seven other spirits more wicked than itself,

> and they go in and live there. And the final condition of that person is worse than the first. That is how it will be with this wicked generation."
> **Matthew 12:43-45 (NIV)**

> Therefore, I urge you, brothers and sisters, in view of God's mercy, to offer your bodies as a living sacrifice, holy and pleasing to God—this is your true and proper worship. Do not conform to the pattern of this world, but be transformed by the renewing of your mind. Then you will be able to test and approve what God's will is—his good, pleasing and perfect will. **Romans 12:1-2 (NIV)**

After submission and deliverance, God starts to reconstruct our lives into a pattern that pleases Him, aligns with His purpose and serve our own best interests. But this happens as a process it will take some time for all the traces of living many years in sin to be removed from our lives. This process demands a continuous walk with God, as we constantly follow the leading of His Spirit and obey His word. It will require humility and obedience as the light of God shines on aspects of our lives and we have to bring those parts of us into agreement with the Word of God.

> Watch and pray so that you will not fall into temptation. The spirit is willing, but the flesh is weak. **Matthew 26:41 (NIV)**

The process of moving steadily away from whom we used to be and into who God is forming us to be is what is the Bible calls spiritual growth. However, spiritual growth is not merely a matter of altering our outward behaviors and external appearance; it is about changing from the heart by attacking the root causes of our past lifestyles. Spiritual growth must be the result of spiritual development. Real change happens when we are transformed at the level of our values, emotions, self-concept and psychological hurts. This level of change requires the power of God to reach into our psyche to uproot the injuries, memories and beliefs, in order to bring inner healing.

> Rend your heart and not your garments. Return to the Lord your God, for he is gracious and compassionate, slow to anger and abounding in love, and he relents from sending calamity. **Joel 2:13 (NIV)**

> Create in me a pure heart, O God, and renew a steadfast spirit within me. **Psalm 51:10 (NIV)**

> You were taught, with regard to your former way of life, to put off your old self, which is being corrupted by its deceitful desires; to be made new in the attitude of your minds; and to put on the new self, created to be like God in true righteousness and holiness. **Ephesians 4:22-24 (NIV)**

Inner Healing

All sin begins as a legitimate need, but that legitimate need becomes a sin because but it was pursued through illegitimate means. As an example; in the book of Genesis, the desire of Eve to be like God was legitimate because when God created humankind, He said 'Let Us make man in our own Image.' Therefore, Eve's desire to be like the Creator was totally in line with His purpose for creating her. But her desire to be like God became sin when it translated into a desire to become God. To be like God is to share His nature, but to become God is to take

His position. The second desire means that we want to become the be-all and end-all of our own existence. God has no say in our decisions and actions. That is a sin.

Therefore, the desire for sexual intimacy and fulfillment is not a sin, but the pursuit of that desire outside the boundaries of a heterosexual marriage relationship is a sin. The need for financial security is not a sin but to become materialistic and make money the most important thing in our lives is a sin. The desire for social relevance, success and recognition are not sins but to be drawn by these desires into living without principles is a sin. All the above desires are legitimate desires which God placed in the human heart. But just as He put those desires in us, He also created the right paths for their pursuit.

Thus, the pursuit of a legitimate God-given desire can actually turn out to be sinful if the motives for wanting them, as well as the methods for reaching them are examined. The keys to understanding the things which have held power over us can be found when we examine why we want the things we want. Why does something become so important that we would do anything to get it? How is it that all other considerations become unimportant and we become ready to hurt people and even ourselves to get that thing? What happened to make it the principal factor that we use in defining who we are and determining our self-worth?

The Spirit of God wants to peel back the hidden reasons behind our actions and desires. He wants to reveal the hidden meanings we attach to things and relationships. He wants to unveil the unseen forces of things we suffered, as well as things we were denied working silently inside to frame our behavior. God wants to reveal the roots of our compulsive behavior and twisted notions. In doing this, He not only brings us to the point of greater self-knowledge, He also wants us to become aware of the how these forces work inside us, so that we become better equipped to manage our lives. By showing us the door through which our trouble entered, He empowers us to guard that door.

> He gives me new strength [renews my soul]. He leads me on paths that are right [righteous; or straight] for the good [sake] of his name [reputation].
> **Psalm 23:3 (EXB)**

There are two main areas where the Spirit of God wants to heal our hearts:

- Our pains and
- Our passions

He wants to heal us in the areas of things that have been done to us or denied us. These are actions and words from other people that wounded our spirits and left scars which have rendered us incapable of living as we should. He also wants to heal us in the area of our passions; these are the wrong desires that rule our hearts. They are cravings; uncontrollable hunger and thirst that draws us to drink from whatever sources happen to be at close at hand. These are usually the habits and impulses that rule and ruin us.

Healing Our Pains

Abuse becomes a force that outlives the duration of the actual events. It keeps on hurting the abused person and locks them into behaving in some negative manner years after they have left the abusive relationship and environment. The effects of the incidents also keep spreading its poison into other areas of the person until their whole life is dominated by the memories and emotions of those incidents. Negative incidents in the past can reach into the future and distort a person's soul totally out of proportion to the original occurrence. This is particularly true if the abuse occurred during our formative years, childhood and teenage years, or if the abuser was someone we invested a lot of emotions in. Hurts we experience inflict deep psychological pains that bind our souls and impair our ability to function properly. They hobble our spirits and leave us limping through life; unable to function properly in our relationship with other people.

> Turn to me and be gracious to me, for I am lonely and afflicted. Relieve the troubles of my heart and free me from my anguish. Look on my affliction and my distress and take away all my sins. **Psalm 25:16-18 (NIV)**

The past can have a grip on the future to the extent that people long dead or forgotten continue to be the dominant force in our destinies. As a result, we are not operating according to the realities of the moment but from our recollections of the past. We do not take advantage of opportunities, recognize our potential or pursue our destinies. We are locked into destructive habits and relationships, constantly sabotaging our chances for success and happiness through our own compulsive behaviors. And the worst thing about being in this situation is that we are not even aware of the source of the things that we do. We may realize that we have trust issues, are unstable in relationships, have a habit of attracting and accommodating losers, always insist on being right, cannot stand to be alone even if it means being in an abusive relationship, cannot keep a job, and tend toward violent conduct. But we cannot pinpoint the point where these attitudes entered our lives or why.

Until we identify the roots of a problem, we cannot truly solve it. Whatever solutions we apply will be short-lived and inadequate. They never bring us to a place of complete freedom; rather we are caught up in cosmetic solutions that merely conceal the problem. The root of the behavior remains and keeps generating the emotion that drives the actions. The person cannot rest but must constantly watch themselves to make sure that they do not lose control. If someone has a tendency to say hurtful things to others, teaching them to control the impulse does not solve the problem. They may stop acting that way for a while, but the anger which causes the behavior remains. One day they will get into a situation that forces the repressed emotions to surface. Then they may believe that they can never change and abandon any attempts to.

> He heals the brokenhearted and binds up their wounds. **Psalm 147:3 (NIV)**

The road to real and lasting change is through introspection and self-revelation in the presence of the Holy Spirit. To reach an understanding of the full impact of abuse on our lives, the following are the steps to take.

Revisit The Events

Although difficult, it is necessary sometimes to relive the events that have caused us the greatest hurts, in order to get to healing. If those events still have a damaging hold on us, it will be revealed in the freshness of its graphics and the intensity of our emotional reactions. There are times when we believe that we have gone past the hurts in our past, when in reality all we have done is buried them out of sight beneath a mass of activities and a mask of normalcy. We think that by avoiding it, we can also evade its impact. But the pain remains inside us, retains its potency and is insidiously destroying us.

> They said to one another, "Surely we are being punished because of our brother. We saw how distressed he was when he pleaded with us for his life, but we would not listen; that's why this distress has come on us." Reuben replied, "Didn't I tell you not to sin against the boy? But you wouldn't listen! Now we must give an accounting for his blood." They did not realize that Joseph could understand them, since he was using an interpreter. He turned away from them and began to weep, but then came back and spoke to them again. He had Simeon taken from them and bound before their eyes. **Genesis 42:21-24 (NIV)**

Joseph had grown past the events of his past and forgotten all about them. But coming face-to-face with those who had hurt him and hearing the things they did to him discussed unleashed a flood of emotions he had not realized were there. The incident had Joseph acting in ways that were totally uncharacteristic of the person he had become. This happened because he had not yet come to a place of complete healing.

Review The Event

Pain has a way of warping our point of view. This is especially true when the abuser is in a position of authority and can impose their interpretation of the events on us. We can go forward without a clear understanding of what happened to us and accept blame where we were only victims. It is not at all uncommon for abused people to blame themselves for the abuse, because it is hard for us to accept our own powerlessness in the situation. We replay the events in our memory, somehow wishing we had possessed the strength to protect ourselves. Over time, that feeling crystallizes into self-blame and excusing abusive behavior. This is one of the reasons people continue to permit themselves to be abused in dysfunctional relationships; they take responsibility for other people's irresponsibility.

> But if out in the country a man happens to meet a young woman pledged to be married and rapes her, only the man who has done this shall die. Do nothing to the woman; she has committed no sin deserving death. This case is like that of someone who attacks and murders a neighbor. **Deuteronomy 22:25-26 (NIV)**

> The king sang this lament for Abner: "Should Abner have died as the lawless die? Your hands were not bound; your feet were not fettered. You fell as one falls before the wicked." And all the people wept over him again. **2 Samuel 3:33-34 (NIV)**

Putting the events that happened to you in their proper context will free you to direct your action to what lies within your power to change.

Accept Your Grief and Loss

Another way people respond to abuse is to deny the impact of that person's actions on them. We try to keep a stiff upper lip;

appear strong and move on. Sometimes people feel a need to act normal and stay in denial because the pain is just too hard to confront or acknowledge. Other times, it is their way of getting back at the abuser and showing them that they have not broken by the act. But because we did not grieve or were not allowed to grieve, we do not give ourselves the chance to heal. Grief must precede healing. Without grief, there is nothing to heal. We may resort to acting like this because we were denied the right to grieve by those who should have comforted us. But that only allows it to fester inside us. Not being allowed to grieve and not being properly comforted, affects the value we place on ourselves. It tells us that maybe we are not just that valuable and should not burden other people with our troubles. A crying child needs attention in order to feel alright. In the same way, when others acknowledge our pain, it facilitates the healing of our hearts.

> When Job's three friends, Eliphaz the Temanite, Bildad the Shuhite and Zophar the Naamathite, heard about all the troubles that had come upon him, they set out from their homes and met together by agreement to go and sympathize with him and comfort him. When they saw him from a distance, they could hardly recognize him; they began to weep aloud, and they tore their robes and sprinkled dust on their heads. Then they sat on the ground with him for seven days and seven nights. No one said a word to him, because they saw how great his suffering was. **Job 2:11-13 (NIV)**
>
> So David and his men wept aloud until they had no strength left to weep. **1 Samuel 30:4 (NIV)**

> The Lord is close to the brokenhearted and saves those who are crushed in spirit. **Psalm 34:18 (NIV)**

Forgive Yourself and Others

Forgiving somebody who hurt you benefits you more than it does them. By refusing to forgive somebody, you also refuse to let go of the event; you keep reliving it along with its pain. It is necessary to keep the hurts fresh in your mind when you do not forgive someone; it arms you with anger and hate against the person. Additionally, you have to play the role of the policeman and judge over their lives, as you constantly watch them, waiting for them to suffer misfortune. But this is no way to live, the incessant preoccupation with that person saps your energy and holds you back. Forgiveness will release you to move on with your life.

Additionally, abuse has a way of making the abused person abusive. Abused People Abuse People. They transfer the negative emotions of the abuse into their relationships with others and hurt them just as they have been hurt. Some abuse victims will actually abuse others in the same ways that they were abused. As a result, the victim becomes united with the villain in doing the same thing. We may justify ourselves by blaming the person who abused us for our actions. Just as they too may blame somebody in their lives for the things that they did to us. Regardless of the reasons for anyone's abusive behavior, the victim of abuse feels its impact just as much. Our excuses do not make our actions less abusive.

> Get rid of all bitterness, rage and anger, brawling and slander, along with every form of malice. Be kind and compassionate to one another, forgiving

> each other, just as in Christ God forgave you. **Ephesians 4:31-32 (NIV)**

> For if you forgive other people when they sin against you, your heavenly Father will also forgive you. But if you do not forgive others their sins, your Father will not forgive your sins. **Matthew 6:14-15 (NIV)**

Just as important as forgiving others is the need to forgive ourselves. If the person who hurt another should be forgiven, how much more should the person they hurt forgive themselves? How do we know that we have not forgiven ourselves? When our hearts constantly harbor guilt and shame or we think we have to do something to earn approval and acceptance.

> He does not treat us as our sins deserve or repay us according to our iniquities. For as high as the heavens are above the earth, so great is his love for those who fear him. **Psalm 103:10-11 (NIV)**

Release The Hurts

Cast ourselves on God and ask Him to heal us. Our goal is to leave the presence of God without the burden of the events. We are not trying to, forget; we just need for it to lose its hold on us. So that we stop grieving all over again; every time we remember the event. Rather, when we are fully healed, we remember the events of our life with a sense of detachment - as if they happened to somebody else. The memories are not so graphic anymore and along with it the pain has disappeared.

> Heal me, Lord, and I will be healed; save me and I will be saved, for you are the one I praise. **Jeremiah 17:14 (NIV)**

> Lord my God, I called to you for help, and you healed me...You turned my wailing into dancing; you removed my sackcloth and clothed me with joy, that my heart may sing your praises and not be silent. Lord my God, I will praise you forever. **Psalm 30:2 (NIV)**
>
> You will surely forget your trouble, recalling it only as waters gone by. **Job 11:16 (NIV)**

Healing Our Passions

God also wants to heal us in the twisted ways we perceive and pursue our passions. As previously noted, our needs may be legitimate but if we go about them in the wrong ways, they become sin. Part of our problem stems from the excessive importance that we place on things. We give them a position in our lives that is disproportionate to the actual value that they provide. The primary areas where passions and misconduct rule the hearts of people are; money and success, social status and power, sex and relationships. God wants to bring us back into balance and center us on Him and not on ourselves, people or things. In doing this, he leads us to a review of the reasons that we want the things we pursue. Sometimes in order to come to the place of truth, we have to give up pursuits, pleasures and relationships.

Sex and Relationships

Relationships with people form the basis of our happiness and wellbeing. Given this fact, people adopt all manner of techniques to keep others in their lives. They do not do this because they value people and want to benefit them. Rather they want to derive some advantage for themselves, even if they provide none to the other person. People want other people because they need company, conversation, sex, fun or respectability. They may not care about reciprocating in ways that keeps the other person happy, but merely use them as tools for their own pleasure. This is why so many people are manipulative and selfish in their relationships.

Other people have no sense of self and cannot live without someone in their lives. Relationships become their primary source of validation; from which they derive meaning, happiness and stability. Without someone in their lives they feel empty and useless. As a result, they will do anything just to be with someone, anyone. In order to keep those people in their lives, they permit abuse from others, become abusive themselves, violate commonsense and sabotage the other person's attempts to be an individual.

These two types of behavior are off-center; God wants us to value people but not to live by them or abuse them

> This is what the Lord says: "Cursed is the one who trusts in man, who draws strength from mere flesh and whose heart turns away from the Lord. **Jeremiah 17:5 (NIV)**

> Let no debt remain outstanding, except the continuing debt to love one another, for whoever loves others has fulfilled the law. **Romans 13:8 (NIV)**

> For they loved human praise more than praise from God. **John 12:43 (NIV)**

Status and Recognition

Directly connected to the way we view people is the way we go about seeking status and recognition. For some people all that matters is what people think about them. The only thing worth having is popularity and fame, and for these they sacrifice family, health and values. If earning respect is the most important thing in our lives, our lives will be lived as a public performance. This is why many young men in the ghettos get drawn into gangs, drugs and crime. They want to earn the respect of their peers and enemies. But status that is derived from the approval of people is fragile. If we live to gain applause and approval from people, we unknowingly trap ourselves. We no longer determine how we live but have transferred power to the audience, and since people are so changeable, their lives become unstable. This is why many celebrities and politicians have no personal values or fixed identity; they are for sale to the largest crowd.

> Fear of man will prove to be a snare, but whoever trusts in the Lord is kept safe. **Proverbs 29:25 (NIV)**

> Then Saul said to Samuel, "I have sinned. I violated the Lord's command and your instructions. I was afraid of the men and so I gave in to them. **1 Samuel 15:24 (NIV)**

Money and Success

Excessive pursuit of money is the disease of our times. Everything is valued in by how much it costs or what it is worth, including people. Because money is the highest value of our society, we give it attention as the surest route to gaining the attention of people. The problem is that the people we impress with our money are often those who do not care about us. And those who hurt the most from our reckless pursuit of material things are those who love us. Money and success distort our vision of ourselves, other people, our relationships and things that actually matter. We know that money is just an illusion yet cannot stop chasing it because we have tied our identity and self-worth to it. Until we bring money back to the place where it is a tool, it will continue to exercise its power to disrupt our lives.

> Then he said to them, "Watch out! Be on your guard against all kinds of greed; life does not consist in an abundance of possessions." **Luke 12:15 (NIV)**
>
> For the love of money is a root of all kinds of evil. Some people, eager for money, have wandered from the faith and pierced themselves with many griefs. **1 Timothy 6:10 (NIV)**
>
> Turn my heart toward your statutes and not toward selfish gain. Turn my eyes away from worthless things; preserve my life according to your word. **Psalm 119:36-37 (NIV)**

INTERLUDE 2: MY STORY

Deliverance and Healing

As I was going through the processes of inner healing and deliverance, God played a tape recorder of my past life to me and I did not like what I saw. I saw someone who made terrible choices, lived in sin and choose the wrong paths in life to get the things I wanted. I did not like the reflection of myself that I saw in the mirror and I repented to GOD. It saddens me deeply to know that I might have hurt others without realizing the impact my actions had on their lives. I often hear people say that we reap what we sow, but the reality is that we will reap a lot more than we sow. It is the truth and I am a living witness of this.

> Do not be deceived: God cannot be mocked. A man reaps what he sows. Whoever sows to please their flesh, from the flesh will reap destruction; whoever sows to please the Spirit, from the Spirit will reap eternal life. **Galatians 6:7-8 (NIV)**

As God was healing me, I examined my family history - three generations back, and I learned why I was struggling with some of the same bondage that many of my family members struggle with today. My mom was rejected and broken as a young child. She became a teenager and had me at an early age. My mother was unknowingly broken; she brings me into the rejection, bitterness, unforgiveness, hurt, depression, and destructive relationships she was experiencing. These things passed on to me through her womb. They didn't start with her, but she inherited it from her mother, and her mother from her mother's mother, and on and on, until it goes back to one hundred years of brokenness and family dysfunctions.

> Maintaining love to thousands, and forgiving wickedness, rebellion and sin. Yet he does not leave the guilty unpunished; he punishes the children and their children for the sin of the parents to the third and fourth generation. **Exodus 34:7 (NIV)**

> Our ancestors sinned and are no more, and we bear their punishment. **Lamentations 5:7 (NIV)**

Through my brokenness, God brought me to a local church where they taught God's Word about inner healing, deliverance, generational curses, Divine healing, spiritual warfare, the true meaning of praise & worship, Baptism in the Holy Spirit, speaking in the spirit and so much more. Through the teachings on deliverance and inner healing, I learned that Christ was made a curse so I could be freed from the curses that sin had brought on me. And that once I accepted Him as my lord and savior, the transfer of bondage from my ancestors through these generational curses would stop. I would no longer be subject to spiritual bondage from my parents once I accepted Jesus!

> Christ hath redeemed us from the curse of the law, being made a curse for us: for it is written, Cursed is every one that hangeth on a tree: **Galatians 3:13 (AKJV)**

After I came to know what my generational curses were and discovered the roots of my past ungodly behavior, I learned that Jesus has given me spiritual authority over demon spirits, and that by faith I could command them to leave in Jesus' name.

Interlude 2: My Story

I also learned of the power in my verbal confessions and that not only was I free, but my generations after me, would be free too. Attending deliverance sessions, I was taught the different tactics the devil has been using to try and destroy God's destiny and purpose for my life and turn it to his wicked purpose instead. I found that deliverance is the children's bread and knew I needed it to be set free.

My faith still gets attacked by the enemy, but I'm so thankful that I am knowledgeable of how to engage in spiritual warfare against his tactics and claim authority over my life and family daily in prayer.

CHAPTER SIX
GRACE THROUGH HUMILITY

The most important personal quality for progressing from brokenness to wholeness is humility. At the core of all of God's dealings with us is the quality of humility, that is the ability to recognize ourselves as dust and Him as God, and note the distance between what we are and who He is. Once that understanding is firmly fixed in our minds and hearts, our response to God becomes founded more on truth than on our fantasies. Humility is the gateway to whatever place God has reserved for us because it helps us to first see ourselves, shortcomings and needs. Then it helps us to see God – His power and provision. Without humility, we cannot see ourselves as deficient and, therefore, cannot view God as sufficient. Our humility is the most important criterion that God uses to judge whether or not, we qualify for His blessings.

> I have a message from God in my heart concerning the sinfulness of the wicked: There is no fear of God before their eyes. In their own eyes they flatter themselves too much to detect or hate their sin.
> **Psalm 36:1-2 (NIV)**

> But these people have stubborn and rebellious hearts; they have turned aside and gone away. They do not say to themselves, 'Let us fear the Lord our God, who gives autumn and spring rains in season, who assures us of the regular weeks of harvest.'

> Your wrongdoings have kept these away; your sins have deprived you of good. **Jeremiah 5:23-25 (NIV)**

Without humility, it is impossible to ask for anything. This is why the ungodly do not pray. To pray would be to acknowledge that you are not enough. And the moment you begin to ask in prayer, the same moment you begin to subject yourself to whatever conditions the one you pray to will impose on you. This is one of the reasons people do not pray, because prayer immediately confers superiority and authority to the one we pray to. That person has the right to dictate the terms because the one praying needs the one to whom he prays, but the reverse is not true. Without humility, we cling to our fantasy of self-sufficiency because we do not want to submit.

> Some became fools through their rebellious ways and suffered affliction because of their iniquities. They loathed all food and drew near the gates of death. Then they cried to the Lord in their trouble, and he saved them from their distress. He sent out his word and healed them; he rescued them from the grave. Let them give thanks to the Lord for his unfailing love and his wonderful deeds for mankind. Let them sacrifice thank offerings and tell of his works with songs of joy. **Psalm 107:17-22 (NIV)**

Without humility, it is impossible to change. This is because in order to go into the new, we must reject the old. To even become aware of the existence of the new, we must listen. And listening is very difficult. Most times when it seems like we are listening, we merely wait for the other person to finish so we can go on with our lives. Or we are compiling our arguments against whatever it is they are saying. People never listen because in a debate what is at stake is not just the points over which we disagree but our status. We really do not defend the things we believe when we argue with somebody; we mostly assert our competence, superiority and power. Arguments are not intellectual, contests; they are power struggles.

> And no one after drinking old wine wants the new, for they say, 'The old is better.' **Luke 5:39 (NIV)**

> Teach me, and I will be quiet; show me where I have been wrong. **Job 6:24-26 (NIV)**

> Teach me your way, Lord; lead me in a straight path because of my oppressors. **Psalm 27:11 (NIV)**

The biggest obstacle to our deliverance, happiness and prosperity is our sense of self-sufficiency, a lack of humility. This is why Satan invests heavily in ensuring that we possess the opposite quality to humility, which is pride. Pride not only makes us inaccessible to God, it makes God antagonistic toward us. God begins to view us as enemies. Pride is the chief sin because it sets us against God. A proud heart stands in opposition to God because it does not merely violate the will of God, like other sins do. Pride actively opposes the person and position of God. Pride does not disobey the word of God, it attacks the throne of God; it refuses to recognize His existence and authority but attempts to take His place.

> The fool says in his heart, "There is no God." They are corrupt, and their ways are vile; there is no one who does good. **Psalm 53:1 (NIV)**

> "Their feet are swift to shed blood; ruin and misery mark their ways, and the way of peace they do not

know." "There is no fear of God before their eyes."
Romans 3:15-18 (NIV)

Every government in the world has laws and various degrees of punishment for breaking its laws. But the government might show leniency against people who break the law, if they demonstrate remorse or provide evidence that the crime was committed in error and ignorance. However, every government reacts with maximum force against crimes it perceives as targeted against it and not its laws. Such crimes, referred to as treason, attempt to unseat the government. They question its legitimacy and undermine its power, and as such attract the full weight of its power. Even when its citizens engage in treasonable acts, the government does not defend itself with the police but uses military force, because treason is a declaration of war.

The same applies with pride; all other sins hurt people and disobey God's laws but pride tries to erase Him. Pride is not just about making a, mistake; it is about challenging God. This is why God has to resist the proud; proud people do not even acknowledge God, much less obey Him. Pride is the chief sin which gave birth to the original sin of rebellion. Before Satan rebelled against God, he first became proud, full of Himself to the point that he decided to dispose of God. He asked why he and the other Angels should worship God and then decided that he also deserved to be worshipped like God. Finally, he led an insurrection against God.

> You were in Eden, the garden of God; every precious stone adorned you: carnelian, chrysolite and emerald, topaz, onyx and jasper, lapis lazuli, turquoise and beryl. Your settings and mountings were made of gold; on the day you were created they

were prepared. You were anointed as a guardian cherub, for so I ordained you. You were on the holy mount of God; you walked among the fiery stones. You were blameless in your ways from the day you were created till wickedness was found in you. So I drove you in disgrace from the mount of God, and I expelled you, guardian cherub, from among the fiery stones. Your heart became proud on account of your beauty, and you corrupted your wisdom because of your splendor. **Ezekiel 28:13-17 (NIV)**

How you have fallen from heaven, morning star, son of the dawn! You have been cast down to the earth, you who once laid low the nations! You said in your heart, "I will ascend to the heavens; I will raise my throne above the stars of God; I will sit enthroned on the mount of assembly, on the utmost heights of Mount Zaphon. I will ascend above the tops of the clouds; I will make myself like the Most High." But you are brought down to the realm of the dead, to the depths of the pit. **Isaiah 14:12-15 (NIV)**

Then war broke out in heaven. Michael and his angels fought against the dragon, and the dragon and his angels fought back. But he was not strong enough, and they lost their place in heaven. The great dragon was hurled down—that ancient serpent called the devil, or Satan, who leads the whole world astray. He was hurled to the earth, and his angels with him. **Revelation 12:7-9 (NIV)**

We may say that we do not have the pride of Satan but once we have a proud spirit, the operations of pride are at work inside our soul and we will also set ourselves against God. We may not lead a revolution against God, but we can deny His influence and authority over us. When somebody refuses to acknowledge that they were made by God, they have figuratively unseated Him. When somebody does not recognize the hand of God working in their successes and achievements, they have taken the place of God as the power that rules their universe. When somebody does not submit to the opinions of God, they have assumed a position as the source and summit of all knowledge.

> For who makes you different from anyone else? What do you have that you did not receive? And if you did receive it, why do you boast as though you did not? **1 Corinthians 4:7 (NIV)**

The rebellion of Satan is not repeated merely by those people who literally reject God; it is also being replayed in the life of anyone who claims for themselves any position that should be reserved for God. They do not pray – they claim all power and complete knowledge, so they see no need to ask for the help of the Almighty. They worship their own abilities and endowments – their intelligence, beauty, strength, wealth and success. They do not give Him thanks – acknowledge that it has not all been by their power but something beyond them has helped them. They demand worship – view themselves as special and superior to the common man. If these are present in any person, they are in the stead of Satan and will attract God's anger.

> If anyone thinks they are something when they are not, they deceive themselves. **Galatians 6:3 Version (NIV)**
>
> All this happened to King Nebuchadnezzar. Twelve months later, as the king was walking on the roof of

the royal palace of Babylon, he said, "Is not this the great Babylon I have built as the royal residence, by my mighty power and for the glory of my majesty?" Even as the words were on his lips, a voice came from heaven, "This is what is decreed for you, King Nebuchadnezzar: Your royal authority has been taken from you. You will be driven away from people and will live with the wild animals; you will eat grass like the ox. Seven times will pass by for you until you acknowledge that the Most High is sovereign over all kingdoms on earth and gives them to anyone he wishes." **Daniel 4:28-32 (NIV)**

"Then he said, 'This is what I'll do. I will tear down my barns and build bigger ones, and there I will store my surplus grain. And I'll say to myself, "You have plenty of grain laid up for many years. Take life easy; eat, drink and be merry."' "But God said to him, 'You fool! This very night your life will be demanded from you. Then who will get what you have prepared for yourself?' "This is how it will be with whoever stores up things for themselves but is not rich toward God." **Luke 12:18-21 (NIV)**

The Nature and Roots of Pride

Pride is that attitude which leads people to promote themselves illegitimately. A proud heart refuses to be subjected to authority, order and process. But arbitrarily chooses what it feels is its due position. Not because of proven competence or apparent results but out of a bloated sense of self-importance. As long as pride holds sway over a person's heart, their feet will be fixed firmly on the path to destruction. This is because their attitudes stand guard against any attempts to have them examine their lives – it prevents them from hearing God. The proud person is spiritually deaf; they are insensitive to God's attempts to help them and as such cannot receive His grace. Therefore, pride is the jailer that keeps guard over people's hearts.

It is the first enemy that God has to deal with before he can begin to address the issues of our lives; it is a stronghold. As long as we are proud Satan's works remain in place in our lives. The wrong thoughts and actions of our lives go unchallenged. The only way that God ever reaches the proud is through disaster. Only then are they forced to stop and consider their ways. Like ants drawn to sugar, so trouble and calamity draw themselves to the proud. There are two sources from which these come; one source is the natural consequence of the person's action and the other is the obstacles that God throws in the person's paths, either to resist them as an enemy or to bring them to a place where they can be corrected.

> Whoever remains stiff-necked after many rebukes will suddenly be destroyed—without remedy. **Proverbs 29:1 (NIV)**

> A person's own folly leads to their ruin, yet their heart rages against the Lord. **Proverbs 19:3 (NIV)**

What is at the root of pride?

Ironically, pride takes its source from a heart that is plagued by fear and a sense of inadequacy. The fear that we are not enough and that other people might discover it or may even suspect it, is what leads to prideful. People strive to be seen, heard and recognized, because they fear that if they do not do so they may be overlooked. They are not so fully assured of who they are that they could afford to let anyone forget it for a moment. The person's hold on what they have and who they are is not strong enough to withstand doubt and obscurity. They actually lack confidence in themselves and attempt to drown out the fear by making a lot of noise. They need to have positions because to not have them would confirm what they feared about themselves.

> Do not exalt yourself in the king's presence, and do not claim a place among his great men; **Proverbs 25:6 (NIV)**

> For those who exalt themselves will be humbled, and those who humble themselves will be exalted. **Matthew 23:12 (NIV)**

If a person is totally confident in what they have or who they are, people's refusal to acknowledge him/her does not diminish them, because they are in full possession of their goods. This is why a wise person can tolerate being considered a fool; they know that their words will eventually win the day. A person who is truly rich is not afraid of wearing clothes or eating food that is for the poor, because it does not affect their worth. That is why a good leader can stoop to doing menial work; it does not make them a servant. This is also why adults who are truly mature can play like little children. And strong people are not afraid to be weak. The proud person's power and status lack substance, so they cannot allow them to be challenged.

> Who is like the Lord our God, the One who sits enthroned on high, who stoops down to look on the heavens and the earth? He raises the poor from the dust and lifts the needy from the ash heap; **Psalm 113:5-7 (NIV)**

> In your relationships with one another, have the same mindset as Christ Jesus: Who, being in very nature God, did not consider equality with God something to be used to his own advantage; rather, he made himself nothing by taking the very nature of a servant, being made in human likeness.
> **Philippians 2:5-7 (NIV)**

Prideful behavior is one of the inevitable consequences of living in an environment where human value is expressed and measured in terms of money. When what counts are only things that can be counted, people will replace people with possessions and positions. We become performance oriented and insane with compulsive acquisitive behavior. People stop wanting stuff because of what it can do for them but because of whom they think it makes them. Things are valued beyond the actual benefits they provide, but for the pleasure of feeding our eyes on them or the envy it generates in the hearts of others. In a society such as this one, it is dangerous to allow yourself to be overlooked. Because who you are depends on what you own and what you own is known by what you show.

> What causes fights and quarrels among you? Don't they come from your desires that battle within you? You desire but do not have, so you kill. You covet but you cannot get what you want, so you quarrel and fight. You do not have because you do not ask God. When you ask, you do not receive, because you ask with wrong motives, that you may spend what you get on your pleasures. **James 4:1-3 (NIV)**

> And I saw that all toil and all achievement spring from one person's envy of another. This too is

> meaningless, a chasing after the wind. **Ecclesiastes 4:4 (NIV)**

This is how we become slaves to the pursuit of material possession and status. We think that the more things we have, the more respect and love we get from people. If people respect us for what we have, then we have to get those things. And when we do get them, we have to shout as loud as we can, so everyone knows who we are. Incidentally we chase things because of people; to be accepted and respected by them. But we never stop to consider that our pursuit is actually destroying people; it is killing us, destroying our relationships and spreading injustice. We are surprised when after we have gained all those things, there is no one who cares enough about us to be impressed by our achievements. There may be those who fear us and those who stay with us to get some of what we have, but almost none who truly love and respect us.

> What good is it for someone to gain the whole world, yet forfeit their soul? **Mark 8:36 (NIV)**

We discover that we have lost people; we have traded our own humanity and the happiness of others for wealth and power. Our family is not there, and the people outside speak of us in uncomplimentary ways. Yet pride prevents us from acknowledging this. When people close to us try to redirect us into actually giving them what they need, namely, more of ourselves, we lash out and accuse them of being selfish – can they not see all the sacrifices we make for them. We actually attempt to manipulate them into feeling guilty about telling us the truth. We delude ourselves into thinking that the people who speak against the lifestyle we have chosen are either lazy or envious of us. We do anything to deny the reality that we are only in pursuit of self-glory; that all our actions have just one motive behind them, the power to dominate others.

What is the evidence of a proud spirit?

Unwillingness to serve

A proud person does not mind work just as long as they can get others to do it. Of course, they will actually appear to serve if it advances their goal of controlling other people. Proud people do not take orders well but know how to give them. In their minds, they are not proud; they are just competent and deserve the position. And it is right for them to be uncooperative when others are in charge, because those other people are inept and do not know what they are doing.

> In the same way, you who are younger, submit yourselves to your elders. All of you, clothe yourselves with humility toward one another, because, "God opposes the proud but shows favor to the humble."
> **1 Peter 5:5 (NIV)**

Will Not Consider Low Things

Proud people consider certain kinds of work or people beneath them. They avoid anything that could affect their carefully cultivated public image – they have to always look nice and smell sweet. Whether it is waiting on tables or changing nappies or helping the elderly, they avoid such work. They may make a lot of noise about their importance but will not lift a finger to do them, except when they want to impress some important people.

> Live in harmony with one another. Do not be proud, but be willing to associate with people of low position. Do not be conceited. **Romans 12:16 (NIV)**

Quickness to Anger

Because a proud person is so conceited, they are quick to take offense. Their image and reputation are paramount to them and anything that merely appears to disregard their status or diminish it, will invoke their anger. Pride and anger go hand in hand, but that anger is not always visible. Many times they will stifle it, just to maintain appearances, but then they go away secretly hating and plotting against the person. Prideful people are spiteful people.

> Whoever is patient has great understanding, but one who is quick-tempered displays folly. **Proverbs 14:29 (NIV)**

Vanity

A proud person feels a need to strut. They are impelled to parade and display their outstanding qualities. This may be money, beauty, physique, intelligence or athleticism. That quality becomes their reason for demanding to be treated like a god. They walk into a room and expect worship. They have become used to the admiration of people and have a condescending attitude toward others, viewing them as only existing to carry out their wishes.

> The eyes of the arrogant will be humbled and human pride brought low; the Lord alone will be exalted in that day. **Isaiah 2:11 (NIV)**

Arrogance

Proud people are showoffs, so they have a need to always be correct or show that they know. This need does not have to be connected to actual knowledge but is based on mere assumptions. Because they believe themselves to be so important, they just think that whatever they think or say must be right, and lesser people have to accept it.

> Though while they live they count themselves blessed - and people praise you when you prosper.
> **Psalm 49:18 (NIV)**

Rebellion

Pride leads people to disregard proper order or constituted authority and attempt to promote themselves on the basis of their success, wealth or beauty. A proud person comes into a church and organization and wants to choose where they ought to seat, what role they should play and expect that people should revere them and defer to them. If they do not get these, they feel insulted and start working against the success of the leader. Proud people have a disruptive influence and create disharmony wherever they go. They do this to put themselves in the center of people's attention, drawing it away from the leader.

> Evildoers foster rebellion against God; the messenger of death will be sent against them. **Proverbs 17:11 (NIV)**

> For rebellion is like the sin of divination, and arrogance like the evil of idolatry. Because you have rejected the word of the Lord, he has rejected you as king." **1 Samuel 15:23 (NIV)**

Excessive Competition

Proud people are constantly comparing themselves with others because they are afraid that somebody might become better than they are. Their pride drives them to want to be the first always, even if they are not the best. This leads them to strife and deceit; they engage in all sorts of behavior to undercut the success of others and retain prominence. Proud people cannot succeed along with others, they are only happy when they are served and worshipped by others.

> Do nothing out of selfish ambition or vain conceit. Rather, in humility value others above yourselves, not looking to your own interests but each of you to the interests of the others. **Philippians 2:3-4 (NIV)**

Obstinate

Because a proud person views themselves as the only voice that should speak in their own life, they do not admit the opinions of other people. As a result, proud people do not take correction easily, if they ever do. Rather than be corrected, they become argumentative. And if they cannot win the argument or are not in a position to argue with that person, they avoid them or become passive aggressive.

> But they did not listen or pay attention; instead, they followed the stubborn inclinations of their evil hearts. They went backward and not forward. **Jeremiah 7:24 (NIV)**

The Power Of Humility

How does a person go from perpetually failing by repeating the same mistakes to a place where they review their lives and redirect their steps? How can anyone execute a U-turn in the ways they think about life, people and money? It is not possible to do this if we are unable to conduct an audit of our lives. This means to carry out a comprehensive and honest reassessment of the direction our life is going in to see if the current path will eventually lead to the destination. But it is not possible to audit our lives without admitting a second or third party and dispassionately listening to their opinions. We cannot change our lives if we do not submit to the scrutiny of another person and accept their rulings.

> Do not be wise in your own eyes; fear the Lord and shun evil. **Proverbs 3:7 (NIV)**

> Search me, God, and know my heart; test me and know my anxious thoughts. See if there is any offensive way in me, and lead me in the way everlasting.
> **Psalm 139:23-24 (NIV)**

People like to say 'do not judge me,' but if we can accept criticism today, we may be able to escape trouble tomorrow. While they are asking others not to judge them, people routinely admit that they do not know everything, yet they also habitually argue about everything and insist that they are right. If you cling to your point of view and keep asserting your own correctness, when will you actually begin to learn the things you admit to not knowing? The fact is this, our knowledge and beliefs are limited to our experiences and environment. There is a whole lot we do not and cannot know, unless someone else points them out to us.

> Jesus said, "If you were blind, you would not be guilty of sin; but now that you claim you can see, your guilt remains. **John 9:41 (NIV)**

> Now this is what the Lord Almighty says: "Give careful thought to your ways. You have planted much, but harvested little. You eat, but never have enough. You drink, but never have your fill. You put on clothes, but are not warm. You earn wages, only to put them in a purse with holes in it." This is what the Lord Almighty says: "Give careful thought to your ways. **Haggai 1:5-7 (NIV)**

Whatever got us to where we are have the power to also keep us there, unless we have the humility to be led in a different path. If you obstinately insist on your own ways, you will also doggedly repeat your old mistakes. Humility allows you to stop for a moment and think and say 'maybe I am wrong.' That momentary pause opens the door to allow you to consider a different point of view. Humans are usually full of their own ways because their minds are occupied with their own arguments. Relinquishing your point of view is hard because it says someone else may be better. But there is nothing wrong with someone being better than you, it's just life. There will always be those who are ahead of you, behind you or equal to you. Would you rather be happy or win an argument and be miserable for the rest of your life?

> Whoever remains stiff-necked after many rebukes will suddenly be destroyed - without remedy.
> **Proverbs 29:1 (NIV)**

> A whip for the horse, a bridle for the donkey, and a rod for the backs of fools! **Proverbs 26:3 (NIV)**

Whatever judges your actions today, helps you escape judgment over your life. Correction alters the course of our lives to ensure that we reach our final destination. This is similar to the flight of an aircraft. For a good portion of its journey, a distance exists between an aircraft's supposed course and its actual direction. Where it is headed does not always coincide with where it is supposed to be going. This difference is often the result of wind, cloud, or the plane's instruments. As a result, the pilot has to do constant course correction to bring the aircraft back on course and guide it to its destination. In the same way, our lives are often hopelessly off course. We get thrown off by our environment, the obstacles we encounter and our personal handicaps. Hence, we need a master navigator to bring us back to the correct path.

> There is a way that appears to be right, but in the end it leads to death. **Proverbs 16:25 (NIV)**

> Then you will understand what is right and just and fair - every good path. For wisdom will enter your heart, and knowledge will be pleasant to your soul. Discretion will protect you, and understanding will guard you. **Proverbs 2:9-11 (NIV)**

By being able to temporarily suspend our own point of view, we save ourselves from future trouble. A wise and experienced person can look at our small actions today and realize their grave impacts on our future. We, on the other hand, have to wait until actions become consequences of recognizing they were wrong. But a person who is wiser and higher than we are can look at what we do today and see what it will cause tomorrow. And God is higher and wiser than we are. By listening to his corrections, we are saved from judgment, getting to a place where we can no longer correct our actions but are consigned to their negative repercussions.

> Even small children are known by their actions, so is their conduct really pure and upright? **Proverbs 20:11 (NIV)**

CHAPTER SEVEN
HUMILITY AND OBEDIENCE

Just as pride is the Jailer that keeps us in Satan's prison, humility is the gateway that ushers us into Christ's riches. What is humility? Humility gets a bad rap most of the time. This is one of the reasons a lot of otherwise good people shun any exhortation that encourages them to be humble. In our culture, humility is hardly discussed and almost has no place in our society. Our guidelines for surviving and thriving in the workplace and relationships are usually antagonistic to the idea of modesty. If we ever talk about being humble, it is usually done as a side note to the main discussion, or we view it as a quality that is good only for decorative purposes; it is no good at helping someone achieve success or power. Are these notions correct?

To understand what humility is, we have to first examine what it is not.

Humility Permits Abuse

Many people view humility as the quality that will make it possible for others to dominate them. They view it as the instrument abusive systems of power, which could be parental, marital, government, work and religious, use to make people easier to control. By taking away the person's voice, the abuser can subjugate their spirit, impose themselves and subject the individual to their will. They feel that humility will rob them of their personality and make them dull and lifeless. The beliefs come from the past where institutions of government, family and religion have used their power to gag and mistreat people; usually by convincing them that being sheepish is being good and that it was the will of God.

Humility is Humiliation

Others view humility as humiliation; it involves the stripping away of all that they love and value. They think that it is not possible to be humble and follow their dreams and aspirations, because humility is irreconcilable with power, wealth and success. They hold an idea that to be humble is to be poor. The unspoken opinion in the hearts of many, including church people, is that being humble will make them weak and vulnerable, a victim of any passing circumstance. And people will perceive them as someone to be bullied, despised and avoided. In essence, the terms in which humility is described to them, makes it appear like the same qualities that they see in those who are failing with their lives. Therefore, they feel humility will make them losers.

Humility is Punishment

Also connected to the above point of view is the belief that humility is retribution. This arises from the fact that we never see contrition and humility in our society except when people get in trouble. Public figures - politicians, business leaders and celebrities – as well criminals appear very humble when they get caught for wrongdoing. It is a quality that offers some advantage if one is faced with the prospect of losing something valuable, such as position, money, and freedom or family. But otherwise, there is no defined place for a humble lifestyle in the society. As such, we view in relation to punishment and trouble, or as useful for manipulating people into believing that we are sorry.

Humility Is Shamefacedness

We believe that a person cannot be humble and still stay joyful and exuberant. Our interpretation of humbleness is acting subdued, looking morose and going around with one's head hanging down in dejection. A truly humble person cannot offer compliments and should not accept them either. But by wearing nondescript clothing and appearing self-effacing, the person properly demonstrates their humility. In other words, not seeing any good in oneself is essential to being humble. This view of humility is repulsive to a lot of people and leads them to reject any exhortation to be humble.

But are these views a true reflection of what it means to be humble? To find an answer we look to our perfect model, Jesus. He said 'I am meek and humble.' But do we find any of the attributes described above in him. And just in case, we feel that Jesus is too far out of reach, He Himself gave us another example of what it is like to be humble. He points us in the direction of little children. He says that if we can understand and acquire the attitudes of little children then we would have gained the qualities to become like Him and access what God has for us.

> Take my yoke upon you and learn from me, for I am gentle and humble in heart, and you will find rest for your souls. **Matthew 11:29 (NIV)**
>
> At that time the disciples came to Jesus and asked, "Who, then, is the greatest in the kingdom of heaven?" He called a little child to him, and placed the

child among them. And he said: "Truly I tell you, unless you change and become like little children, you will never enter the kingdom of heaven. Therefore, whoever takes the lowly position of this child is the greatest in the kingdom of heaven. And whoever welcomes one such child in my name welcomes me.
Matthew 18:1-5 (NIV)

What is Humility?

Humility is the ability to recognize our position in relation to God and assume the right attitude to that reality. Humility says 'I am below but He is above' or 'I am wrong and He is right' or 'I am weak and He is strong' or I am human but He is Divine.' Humility is the quality of being able to regard yourself as you truly are, to view your actions through the lens of truth and allow God's word to cut you back in your excesses. It is the acceptance of our current level of power, knowledge, success and growth, without fretfulness. It is to wholeheartedly accept your place in life and be faithful in it, rather than coveting someone else's place and burning with envy as a result. Humility helps you to be at peace with who you are and not lose your peace trying to create a false appearance in order to impress people.

> For by the grace given me I say to every one of you: Do not think of yourself more highly than you ought, but rather think of yourself with sober judgment, in accordance with the faith God has distributed to each of you. **Romans 12:3 (NIV)**

This is why the Bible describes humility as 'not minding high things.' This does not mean to be without ambition but to be able to enjoy life where you are instead of losing sleep over where you are not. It means to not become too preoccupied with the higher place that you become unable to live in the current place. When a person minds high things, they will do all that is in their power to disguise the fact of where they are. They will become self-promoting and seek advancement at all costs. They will be unable to relate or value people who exist in their current level, having eyes only for those above them. They will become manipulative and materialistic, with their whole lives dedicated to reaching the next level. Humility is to be at peace in a lowly place.

> But when you are invited, take the lowest place, so that when your host comes, he will say to you, 'Friend, move up to a better place.' Then you will be honored in the presence of all the other guests.
> **Luke 14:10 (NIV)**

Humility is also our recognition of God's authority to chastise us, in the same way that children accept their parent's right to discipline them. It is the ability to accept that discipline with the attitude of a child; with no shame, anger or bitterness. Children may cry when they are disciplined but they never feel insulted by their parent's discipline. There is no embarrassment in the child being disciplined by a parent because of the following facts about a child.

The child has no status to defend: There is no feeling of violation because there is no office to defend or reputation to live up to

There is no shame: Children submit themselves to the highest level of scrutiny through their nakedness. They submit their bodies to the parent's inspection without any embarrassment.

<u>There is no private property</u>: Children recognize that the parent needs no permission to look into their belongings. The parent even chooses how the child uses what the child owns.

<u>There is no fear</u>: Children have no need of status and do not suffer from shame because they know that they are accepted by the parent, just as they are. Even if they messed up their clothes, they are accommodated.

<u>There is Love</u>: There are constant acts of validation by the parent as they regularly invest time, money, energy and themselves in the child. The child knows it is loved

<u>There is Trust</u>: The feels that the parent knows better and that discipline is for its own good because the parent has always acted for the child's benefit.

> Endure hardship as discipline; God is treating you as his children. For what children are not disciplined by their father? If you are not disciplined—and everyone undergoes discipline—then you are not legitimate, not true sons and daughters at all. Moreover, we have all had human fathers who disciplined us and we respected them for it. How much more should we submit to the Father of spirits and live! They disciplined us for a little while as they thought best; but God disciplines us for our good, in order that we may share in his holiness. No discipline seems pleasant at the time, but painful. Later on, however, it produces a harvest of righteousness and peace for those who have been trained by it.
> **Hebrews 12:7-11 (NIV)**

We also must become so open to God that we are literally naked in His presence. Although, He knows everything, God would rather be invited into our secret desires and motives, than snoop around to unearth them. He wants His authority in our lives to be accepted willingly, not imposed on us. He wants our status or reputation to cease being an obstacle to our obeying His instructions.

The Effects of Humility

Humility is primarily a change in our view of our personal power, status and importance. It results in a change of disposition toward life as a whole. When we become humble towards God, it will reflect in our relationship with people. The following characteristics manifest in us when humility has found its place in our hearts.

Respect For Other People

Proud people want to determine the position of other people. They will refuse to acknowledge someone in their proper capacity especially if that person has been recently promoted or just became successful. They will insist on relating to the person as they choose, not as their new position dictates. Humility causes a person to respect authority and other people's position and success. The humble person does not feel diminished by the advancement of someone else, and is willing to acknowledge their new status. As a rule, humility makes us more accepting of correction, able to accommodate other people's opinions and be less sensitive to criticism. We will communicate better.

> Submit to one another out of reverence for Christ.
> **Ephesians 5:21 (NIV)**

> In the same way, you who are younger, submit yourselves to your elders. All of you, clothe yourselves with humility toward one another, because, "God opposes the proud but shows favor to the humble."
> **1 Peter 5:5 (NIV)**

Patience

Humility will confer on a person the ability to peacefully wait in line for whatever they desire. A humble person goes past the place of disquiet into the place of peace. This is not out of a sense of complacency but from an attitude of trust and sub-mission. It is not a recipe for laziness but a strategy for finding rest. It is based on the understanding that our abilities are limited in what they can do; that in fretting over what we can do nothing about, we not only lose the moment, we are not moved closer to the future. The attitude comes from the realization that what drives people to do untoward things to gain their desire is the excessive love of money and power. A humble person does all they should do to get what they want, but after that they leave the rest in God's hand. They are able to live with the probability of not eventually getting the things that they desire.

> For there is a proper time and procedure for every matter, though a person may be weighed down by misery. **Ecclesiastes 8:6 (NIV)**
>
> My times are in your hands; deliver me from the hands of my enemies, from those who pursue me.
> **Psalm 31:15 (NIV)**

A Quiet Spirit

A humble person is less noisy inside them. All of the negative thoughts and feelings raging inside their hearts are silenced, and the person acquires a more reserved disposition a quiet outlook toward life. The central factor in the clamor that dominates the heart of the proud is the desire for self-glory; power, recognition, position and domination. Once this is removed, the person loses their appetite for strife. They are able to live their lives peaceably and do their work quietly. They no longer work to be seen and heard; rather they aim to make an impact through the results of their efforts, success.

> And to make it your ambition to lead a quiet life: You should mind your own business and work with your hands, just as we told you. **1 Thessalonians 4:11 (NIV)**

> It is good to wait quietly for the salvation of the Lord. **Lamentations 3:26 (NIV)**

Overlooks Insult

Humility allows us to be overlooked and not get angry. Since the humble person is able to willingly lay down their status, if someone else fails to recognize them, they do not become contentious. The reason a humble person will not call attention to his status is because he/she knows that their power is intact regardless of how somebody treats them. They do not live their lives in the public arena for people's attention and approval. The standard that guides their conduct is the word of God and it is God's attention and approval they always need to have. If a humble person enters a place or organization and is not accorded respect, they do not become resentful and leave, they allow their results and other people speak for them.

> Let someone else praise you, and not your own mouth; an outsider, and not your own lips. **Proverbs 27:2 (NIV)**

> It is not good to eat too much honey, nor is it honorable to search out matters that are too deep. **Proverbs 25:27 (NIV)**

Peace

A humble person has an aversion for conflict and strife. If they are cheated or denied their due, they do not become excessive in their pursuit of their right. It is not prideful to demand what is rightfully ours. But if in trying to get what is ours, our efforts cause us to veer into strife - where we become vengeful, hateful, angry or quarrelsome - then that possession has become a door of pride to enter our lives. That pursuit is an indication of the excessive importance that we place on that thing. To expect recognition and reward for who we are, what we have and what we achieve is well within our rights, but we must not let that right unsettle our spirits and upset our character.

> It is to one's honor to avoid strife, but every fool is quick to quarrel. **Proverbs 20:3 (NIV)**

> If it is possible, as far as it depends on you, live at peace with everyone. **Romans 12:18 (NIV)**

Preferring Others

The prideful person announces themselves, but the humble person waits to be recognized. And beyond waiting to be recognized, a humble person will announce or recognize another person. Rather than struggle for recognition, they will give others recognition. A proud person deprecates others by diminishing their status, criticizing their efforts and minimizing their achievements. Humble people do not do this. That is not to say that the humble person engages in flattery or in blowing other people's trumpet. It only means that when the occasion demands it, they will recognize others and give them their due.

> Be devoted to one another in love. Honor one another above yourselves. **Romans 12:10 (NIV)**

> Do nothing out of selfish ambition or vain conceit. Rather, in humility value others above yourselves. **Philippians 2:3 (NIV)**

Responsiveness

A humble person is more attentive, since they are less tuned into themselves. A humble person is able to listen without presuming that they already know what the other person is going to say. And because a humble person is less defensive and more open to criticism, they are less selfish toward their spouse, children, friends, co-workers and people in general. Humility impacts on our empathy because we no longer seek only what benefits us; we give more consideration to the needs and feelings of others. A humble person brings stability and peace into their relationships. A humble person is a pleasure to have around but even proud people hate the proud.

"A new command I give you: Love one another. As I have loved you, so you must love one another. By this everyone will know that you are my disciples, if you love one another." **John 13:34-35 (NIV)**

Carry each other's burdens, and in this way you will fulfill the law of Christ. **Galatians 6:2 (NIV)**

Teachable

Some people can only learn from people who possess specific credentials; they only respect competence in a certain area of life. If someone does not have experience in that area, they do not believe that the person has any value to impart to them. Humble people, on the other hand, recognize that every person owns or knows something that they do not. Through this understanding they can stoop low enough to be taught even by a child. This makes the humble person far wiser than their breadth of experiences and personal abilities permit. They allow many streams of wisdom into their lives and as such greatly reduce the number of difficulties that they face in life. Wisdom clears a person's path of obstacles.

> Whoever disregards discipline comes to poverty and shame, but whoever heeds correction is honored. **Proverbs 13:18 (NIV)**

> Whoever loves discipline loves knowledge, but whoever hates correction is stupid. **Proverbs 12:1 (NIV)**

Soft Words

Humility teaches our lips how to speak to people. A humble person is less aggressive and not as likely to use words that aggravate people. Humble people know how to choose their words. The words of the pride cause strife and war, but the words of the humble create peace and bring healing. A humble person finds it easy to say 'please.' 'I am sorry' and 'thank you.' Being able to use these words habitually releases benefits that are missing in the experience of proud people.

> A gentle answer turns away wrath, but a harsh word stirs up anger. **Proverbs 15:1 (NIV)**
>
> How forcible are right words! But what doth your arguing reprove? **Job 6:25 (AKJV)**
>
> An honest answer is like a kiss on the lips. **Proverbs 24:26 (NIV)**

Please: Saying please opens doors of favor and gives us access to things that were not originally reserved for us. Telling someone please demonstrates to them that you recognize their power, ownership of the property and rights to say no. It accords them their due recognition.

I Am Sorry: Being able to apologize when you are wrong and even when you are not wrong disarms the strong. It prevents us from engaging in unnecessary wars and makes our lives easier. People who are unable to apologize will stumble against obstacles they could easily avoid.

Thank You: Showing gratitude keeps us under seasons of favor because it keeps the door of blessing perpetually opened to us. A person who knows how to appreciate little things put themselves in position to receive even more, sometimes beyond what they asked.

Why do people speak roughly? Because they think it demonstrates their power and that if they fail to speak back when confronted or insulted, they will be looked upon as weak. But the only thing that this achieves is that we stir up conflict constantly, until the day we stir up a strong and vengeful enemy against ourselves.

INTERLUDE 3: MY STORY

Freedom and Peace

Once, I became free from these generational curses and delivered from the Jezebel spirit of control, the spirit of pride anger, rebellion, disobedience and fear; I started to correctly honoring people regardless of their status. I also let go of past hurt and started practicing forgiveness. I often remind myself that the same way that Christ has forgiven me of my sins, I must also forgive. I began to admit my faults, apologizing for my mistakes and accepting good advice from other people, even if they were not in my social circle.

My new walk in humility brought me to the place where I could walk in obedience, asking others for forgiveness when I was wrong and show respect to people for who they are and not what they had or what I could gain from them. I learned to engage with those who held hate in their hearts and still choose to look upon them with grace and love. I came to value everyone's opinion even when I disagreed, pray for those who disappointed or abandoned me and I also learned to forgive myself.

God is still chiseling me with a hammer daily and molding me into how He wants me to be. I still struggle sometimes with accepting orders from people in authority, especially when I do not think it is fair. However, instead of being rebellious, I have learned to release the situation to God in prayer. I ask him to show me my heart; because I might not be seeing my leader's way clearly and help me to accept it. Then I also ask God to show them their heart.

The outcome of my storms brought about my deliverance, inner healing, and a closer relationship with GOD. I have a better prayer life and I found my purpose and destiny in God's Kingdom. I thank God, every day for the storms and struggles that I encountered and for every tear that I shed; they were well worth the joy, peace, and freedom I have with Him today.

> So if the Son sets you free, you will be free indeed.
> **John 8:36 (NIV)**

CHAPTER EIGHT
HUMILITY, OBEDIENCE AND HEALING

The things that people consistently think and do determine who they become. To leave the current course of our lives, we must consciously set ourselves against the flow of our past lives. We must embark on an upstream course, by taking power away from those things that come easily to us, but take us downhill. We must begin the process of migrating out of the comfort zone into the place of conscious actions. The comfort zone is not a place of intentional choices but habitual actions; we think, speak and act by reflex. There is no examination of the consequences of the action against the desired goal, to see if it is the best way to behave. In the comfort zone, we are creatures of instinct and not beings of insight.

In order to escape from the power of the past, we must start plotting the direction we want to go from here onwards. Rather than allow ourselves to be moved along by trends, popular opinion and our dominant passions, we must carefully choose those thoughts, actions and relationships that reflect the values we now promote. Then we must devise ways to increase their presence and influence in our lives. This is because becoming anything in life is always a matter of what we subject ourselves constantly to. The human spirit is a sponge that absorbs whatever its environment is saturated with. If we live in an environment that is full of cursing, we will soon slip into acting like everyone else around us. Although, it is may be possible to remain different even in that environment, it is a hard and daily battle.

Our lives are the sum of the YES and NO that we say most consistently. All our small decisions and choices become the monumental difficulties and successes we eventually experience. To become the person that God wants us to become, we must find and say YES constantly to the things that reinforce His plans for our lives. As we also say NO to those things we habitually did in the past. The process of change is a constant struggle between the NO and the YES of our lives. The more we yield to the YES of God's word, the more His light enters our lives. But the more we submit to the NO of our past life, the more we regress into darkness. And not only are we saying YES, we are also removing those things that make it hard to YES. We weaken the NO and empower the YES by changing our environment.

This process of going from where evil spirits, negative emotions and wrong people entered our lives and damaged it, to the place where we are protected by God's word is only possible through humility. As the Spirit of God attempts to guide us away from the poisoned waters to a pasture where we are safe and find a beneficial drink, He demands submission. This surrender is a daily habit of constantly giving over our thoughts, actions and relationships to God. It requires a constant study of His word and meditation on the insights we gain to burn their truth into our spirits. It requires the cultivation of a habit of frequent prayer to build resilience into our spirits and enable us to resist our passions, as well as social pressures. In the same way that we became good at wrongdoing by doing it daily, we must become good at doing right by doing it daily.

Leaving Spiritual Infancy

Sometimes this process will resemble the struggle between a mother and her baby as she tries to wean the child. Do any of us remember being weaned? Can we understand why a baby insists on continuing to live on milk? Does it ever cross the child's mind that there is a rich variety of food types and tastes awaiting it in the world? The child cannot understand why the mother denies it sustenance. And no matter what the mother tried to explain to the baby, she just could not make it understand. The mother is therefore left with no other option than to resolutely but gently lead the child away from what it has become used to, towards what it needs to become accustomed to. As adults, it is difficult to understand why as babies we struggled to hold on to milk with its limited options, but as babies, this insight was hidden from us.

The struggle which occurs during the weaning process is not over food because the child will accept other kinds of food as long as it can continue to be breastfed. The struggle is over a psychological attachment to a past level of development and the unwillingness to make the sacrifice necessary to move forward. The child wants the other types of food as long as it does not have to let go of milk. The new is alright as long as there is room for the old. But allowing the baby to do this effectively prevents it from leaving infancy and progressing into adulthood. In the same way, we also want this new life but do not want to give up the old. We reason that those things may not be so bad or that we should take it slowly. But any lingering attachments to the past will reinforce its hold and keep us out of the future.

> But I have calmed and quieted myself, I am like a weaned child with its mother; like a weaned child I am content. **Psalm 131:2 (NIV)**

Letting go is hard because we imagine that by giving up our ways, we are also giving up every chance of getting the things that we want. Just like the baby who has become accustomed to the warmth of the mother's body and feels a sense of loss when it is denied breast milk. We imagine that the ways in which we have pursued our desires are the only ways to reach them; we cannot imagine that our dream could happen any other way. Therefore, if someone took away the methods, they must automatically be taking away the results too. The struggle results from the fear that all hopes of achieving our dreams die when we give up our ways. Because we do not see that our ways have actually kept us from happiness.

> Brothers and sisters, I could not address you as people who live by the Spirit but as people who are still worldly—mere infants in Christ. I gave you milk, not solid food, for you were not yet ready for it. Indeed, you are still not ready. You are still worldly. For since there is jealousy and quarreling among you, are you not worldly? Are you not acting like mere humans?
> **1 Corinthians 3:1-3 (NIV)**

> But solid food is for the mature, who by constant use have trained themselves to distinguish good from evil. **Hebrews 5:14 (NIV)**

As the child becomes subdued by the mother and reconciles itself to the new reality - that it will never live on milk anymore in the same way, we also become humbled and accept the fact that we can no longer live as we did. We submit to this new life and yield to the strange experiences because, like the baby trusts the mother, we have faith in God's love and know that He works all things for our good. Humility is founded on trust and trust draws its strength from our knowledge of God's love. Because we know that He will do us good and not harm, we follow his leadership and tutelage, even if sometimes He leads us to places and through things that are difficult to handle. Faith in His love and character provide the strength to go through.

> The Lord is my shepherd, I lack nothing. He makes me lie down in green pastures, He leads me beside quiet waters, He refreshes my soul. He guides me along the right paths for his name's sake. Even though I walk through the darkest valley, I will fear no evil, for You are with me; your rod and your staff, they comfort me. **Psalm 23:1-4 (NIV)**

Following God

By obeying God and humbling ourselves to be led by His Word and Holy Spirit, we set our feet on an upward spiral of unending growth experiences. Rather than stumbling from one defeat and loss to another defeat and loss, we go from becoming strong in one area of life to becoming strong in another area.

We literally grow 'from strength to strength' in God; becoming more capable in different areas of our lives; emotionally, spiritually, financially and relationally.

> They go from strength to strength, till each appears before God in Zion. **Psalm 84:7 (NIV)**

This cycle of increasing strength comes as we experience different levels of God's grace – we are going 'from grace to grace.'

> Out of His fullness we have all received grace in place of grace already given. **John 1:16 (NIV)**

The overall result of this is that we are released into a life of compounding successes; we move steadily from one level of success and victory to another level of success and victory – 'from glory to glory.'

> And we all, who with unveiled faces contemplate the Lord's glory, are being transformed into his image with ever-increasing glory, which comes from the Lord, who is the Spirit. **2 Corinthians 3:18 (NIV)**

Our newfound experiences overflow into every aspect of our lives.

Our walk with God is progressive. God begins with the changes that we can understand and manage at our level of development and as we continue to follow Him, He leads us into deeper levels of transformation. The key to total transformation is constant submission. People only know the things they want but cannot tell how those things will happen. We usually have no idea of the experiences we need in order to become what we should become or the people who will create our opportunities for success. But by following God and obeying Him, we are led into positively reinforcing environments, beneficial relationships and right actions that unlock our destinies.

We are slowly changed into the person that we need to become; starting at the level of those experiences that have formed our character. Moving on to the ways of behaving we adopted to protect ourselves and get by in life. And finally, He deals with those wrong beliefs and values that we learned from our environments. By following God, we allow Him to carry out a complete reconstruction of our lives, until we are totally different from whom we used to be. But getting to this point requires us to live by certain insights.

> But whoever looks intently into the perfect law that gives freedom, and continues in it - not forgetting what they have heard, but doing it—they will be blessed in what they do. **James 1:25 (NIV)**

Steps To A Transformed Life

In your journey to becoming a new person, the following truths are important to keep in sight.

You Must Build as You Break

It is important that you do not merely focus on the negatives in your life. Do not just attempt to break your old habits, focus much more on forming new ones. You escape an old way of doing things by moving toward a new way. Rather than obsess over what you have done wrong, focus on how to do the right. If you fixate on old habits, you are merely trying to break without building. But when you work toward a new mode of behavior, you simultaneously break and build. There are no free spaces in life; every ground is a territory. When you just attempt to remove a wrong way of behavior without creating a new one, you are trying to create a spiritually neutral ground; you will be frustrated.

> But I will not drive them out in a single year, because the land would become desolate and the wild animals too numerous for you. **Exodus 23:29 (NIV)**

Consistency is The Key

Practicing your chosen new habit daily, in the same way and the same time is the key to changing your behavior. You will gain more ground consistently studying the Bible and praying for thirty minutes every day than you will gain by studying and praying for three hours once a week. It is harder on your flesh to do something, however small, in a consistent manner every day for a considerable length of time. The ability to do something consistently strengthens your ability to say NO. By regularly saying NO in private to laziness, tiredness, apathy, or other excuses, you make it easier to say NO to friends, colleagues and family.

> Go to the ant, you sluggard; consider its ways and be wise! **Proverbs 6:6 (NIV)**

> A sluggard says, "There's a lion in the road, a fierce lion roaming the streets!" As a door turns on its hinges, so a sluggard turns on his bed. **Proverbs 26:13-14 (NIV)**

> The plans of the diligent lead to profit as surely as haste leads to poverty. **Proverbs 21:5 (NIV)**

Focus on habits

Focus on your habits beginning with your thought pattern. We may not realize it but we all have a default mode of thinking that we constantly lapse into. By watching your thoughts, you set a guard over your actions and arrest the negative direction of your life. Failing to start with the though habits will only result in failure. This is why meditating on the word of God is very important; it gives us words and ideas to displace the negative ones that have since occupied our minds. Changing our thought habits will affect our other habits. This is why the though frontier attracts the hardest struggle. In order to change ourselves from the inside we must learn to pray. Prayer breaks the strongholds of our minds. Form habits of studying God's word and praying.

> Like newborn babies, crave pure spiritual milk, so that by it you may grow up in your salvation. **1 Peter 2:2 (NIV)**

> Pray continually. **1 Thessalonians 5:17 (NIV)**

> Seven times a day I praise you for your righteous laws. **Psalm 119:164 (NIV)**

Go into Isolation

In your season of infancy, when you are trying to grasp new ideas or attitudes, it is sometimes necessary to isolate yourself. This does not mean you must go and live on a deserted island in the ocean. It means that you must cut yourself off situations, people and environments that are likely to drag you back into what you are trying to escape. By limiting your exposure to these kinds of influences, you give yourself the space and time to grow. The new direction that you are trying to go in is like a seed that just sprouted; which must be shielded from the wind, weeds and trampling feet. When that seed goes from being a sapling to becoming a tree, it would have built enough shock absorbers to withstand every harmful thing in its environment, and will no longer require protection. In the same way when God took Israel out of Egypt, He isolated them to give Him a chance to mold them without contrary influences.

> What agreement is there between the temple of God and idols? For we are the temple of the living God. As God has said: "I will live with them and walk

among them, and I will be their God, and they will be my people." Therefore, "Come out from them and be separate, says the Lord. Touch no unclean thing, and I will receive you." And, "I will be a Father to you, and you will be my sons and daughters, says the Lord Almighty." **2 Corinthians 6:16-18 (NIV)**

Progress to Insulation

The goal of Isolation is to build insulation into us. When we are isolated, we are kept away from danger. But when we become insulated, we become capable of handling that danger. A point should come in your experience where you are able to enter potential tempting situations in business, the public and in your relationships and still maintain your ground. In the same way that we keep little children away from adult activities until they are old enough to understand them, the goal of isolation is to give us the chance to develop our personal strength in private. So that when we eventually encounter situations in public, we will have the tools to handle them. If we do not progress from isolation to insulation, we will never become a light to the world, since we would have to constantly avoid people who are different from us. As a result, we will never grow into our ministries.

> Neither do people light a lamp and put it under a bowl. Instead they put it on its stand, and it gives light to everyone in the house. In the same way, let your light shine before others, that they may see your good deeds and glorify your Father in heaven.
> **Matthew 5:15-16 (NIV)**

> My prayer is not that you take them out of the world but that you protect them from the evil one.
> **John 17:15 (NIV)**

It Begins With A Decision

The secret to everything that we have ever desired lies with God and the key that unlocks the door to God is humility. The proof of humility is acceptance of His words to us; submission. The proof of submission to his word is obedience. Once we make up our minds to obey God, we have begun the journey out of bondage into becoming blessed. From that first act of humility, submission and obedience, our lives steadily progress away from what had held us down. We do not even know when we are freed from things that had such a grip on us that we never imagined that we would be able to live without them. These may be destructive habits, toxic relationships, demonic oppression and even physical illnesses. But slowly and steadily as we follow God, our lives progress upwards and before we know it we have climbed out of the pit of satanic oppression into lasting freedom.

> This day I call the heavens and the earth as witnesses against you that I have set before you life and death, blessings and curses. Now choose life, so that you and your children may live **Deuteronomy 30:19 (NIV)**

> Consider it pure joy, my brothers and sisters, whenever you face trials of many kinds, because you know that the testing of your faith produces perseverance. Let perseverance finish its work so that you may be mature and complete, not lacking anything. **James 1:2-4 (NIV)**

You may feel today that you need a little more time or have to do just one more thing before you turn your life over to God. But every day spent doing the wrong thing makes the bars of our prison stronger. It makes it harder for us to break free because we feel we have much more to lose and the struggle to liberty is also much harder. By delaying today, you compound your situation and complicate it further. In the same way that doctors are better able to help you if they can catch the disease earlier, God wants you now. Additionally, continuing in the path that you have lived in may bring catastrophe on you. You may suffer a loss that you could never replace. If you wait until your marriage breaks up or someone dies, that is a consequence you can do nothing about but have to live with the rest of your life. If you are reading this, you have a chance to set things right. And you can do that by faithfully praying the prayers in the next section.

CHAPTER NINE

PRAYERS, CONFESSIONS AND DECLARATIONS

Prayer of Humility before God

Dear God, I come to you in the Name of Your Son and my Lord, Jesus Christ. I come without any claims but only by the mercies that come from your grace through Jesus. I recognize that I have lived my life in rebellion against your commands and in violation of your authority. I have acted boastfully and exalted myself unduly. I have spoken arrogantly and willingly disregarded Your truth. I recognize my guilt and accept your judgment against my sins. All that I have suffered have been the due rewards of my pride; I have been wrong but You have been right. But Dear God, Your Word says that if Your people humble themselves and pray and turn from their wrongdoing, that You will hear and heal them. Therefore, I come today, humbling myself without reservation. I place before you my status, my reputation, my boasting and kneel before you in humility. Forgive my rebellion, forgive my arrogance and pride. Deliver me from the consequences of my willfulness and create a humble spirit within me. I turn away from my willful living and I ask you to accept me in the sweet name of Jesus, I pray. Amen.

Prayer to bring Humility to the Heart

Dear Lord, I come to you in my weakness and ignorance. Your Word says that You resist the proud but give grace to the humble. Lord, I want to be humble, so that I can receive your grace but I do not know how to. But Your Word says that You will work in me to will and also to do what you want me to do. Lord, I believe that my willingness to be humble is the proof that you are working in me to be humble. Therefore, I surrender my whole life to the instruction of Your Holy Spirit. Show me the sources and roots of my past behavior and grant me the grace to address and destroy them. Create in me a humble heart; deliver me from a haughty spirit and high mindedness. Teach my lips to be gentle in my speech. Guide me in my relationships to not be judgmental and arrogant. Grant me the humility to serve others and the patience to wait for your will. Father, grant me the ability to not promote myself, but to be willing to accept a lowly position. Lord, above all I ask that you create in me the mind of Christ, so that I can be pleasing to you. This I ask in Jesus Name. Amen.

Prayer to Forgive Others and Yourself

Lord, I just want to thank you for your gift to forgive others and myself. Father God, Your Son Jesus suffered worse than I or anybody can imagine, yet He set an example for us to follow, by forgiving those who hurt Him. Father I come to You today, forgiving (mention the name of the person you want to forgive) for hurting, rejecting, deceiving, cheating, belittling, abusing, and _____ me. I choose to forgive today and I ask you to strip from me any unforgiveness and bitterness from the root of my heart right now, in the Name of Jesus. Father You said that I cannot hate my brother and claim to love you. Therefore, I forgive _____ today; I release and let them go now. I ask you to bless _____. Lord, I also forgive myself of any blame, guilt and shame that I carry. I release the burdens of those painful memories and I surrender to the healing power of your Holy Spirit to wash me of every hurt. I claim wholeness and happiness for myself in the Name of Your Sweet Son Jesus. Amen.

A prayer for Salvation

Dear God, I come to You in the Name of Jesus. Your word says that we all have sinned and fallen short of the just requirements of Your Word. Lord, I come to you as a sinner standing under your righteous judgment and I repent of my sins and I ask for mercy and forgiveness. Dear God, because of your love for me, you sent your Son, Jesus, to suffer in my place by dying on the cross for my sins. Today, I accept the sacrifice of Jesus of Jesus and I ask you to wash my sins away by the blood of your son. Forgive me of my sins and cleanse me from every wrong way of thinking and living; deliver me from the power of sin. I surrender my life to your will and bring everything that belongs to me under your control. Today, I declare that I am no longer the master of my life but I accept Jesus as my savior and the Lord of my life. Lord, erase my name from the book of death and write it in Your book of life. Today, I do declare that I am saved, that I am born again by the blood of Jesus. Dear God, thank you for saving me, in the Name of your sweet Son, Jesus, I pray. Amen.

Prayer for Breaking Generational Curses

Dear God, Your Word says that if I submit myself to You and I resist the Devil, that he will flee from me. Today, I stand in the place of submission and I resist every generational curse in my life, in Jesus name. I address every spirit that connects me to the curses and bondage of my ancestors and I break the chains and links by which they have oppressed me. The word of God says that if a man is in Christ, he is a new creature. The word of God says that Christ has transferred me from the dominion of darkness into the Kingdom of God. Therefore, I declare that I no longer belong to you, Satan, or to any of your monitoring spirits. By the authority vested in me through the Name of Jesus, I declare myself freed. I address every familiar spirit that has been operating in my life and the life of everyone in my house and I cast you out. I command you to leave right now, you have no authority. I declare your powers broken and all your operations ended. I close every door and window by which you have entered our lives and I declare my life, my family and my home, the property of God. Dear god, I give you total control of our lives. Let your Holy Spirit have free rein over our lives and let the blood of Jesus be a hedge around us. All these I declare and affirm in the name of your Precious Son, Jesus. Amen.

Prayer for Prosperity

Dear God, Your Word says that you wish above all things that I prosper and be in health, just as my soul prospers. You have also said to me that I should not worry about what I will eat or drink, because You know that I need these things. Also Your Word says that if I make Your Kingdom my priority, you will give me all other things. Therefore, Lord, on the strength of these promises and scriptures, I come today to the God who owns the silver, the gold and the cattle on a thousand hills. Lord, I ask you to bless me, bless the work of my hand and the place of my dwelling. Lord, let your blessing be upon my mind and I ask that you release to me problem-solving insight and profitable ideas. I also ask that you will fill my heart with wisdom that will impart diligence to my mind and skill to my hands. Lord, lead my feet to cross paths with those whom you have positioned to be a blessing to me and give me favor when they set their eyes on me.

Lord, give me a tongue like that of Daniel that is able to dissolve great difficulties for eminent people. Make me a steward of Your Kingdom, above all, and teach me to honor you with the material things that you give to me and to be a blessing to my family, community, church and nation. All these I pray in the sweet Name of Your Son, Jesus.

ABOUT THE AUTHOR

Yolanda Washington-Cowan is the CEO of B-Inspired Publishing Company, as well as an author under her label.

She is the founder of B-Inspired.Org, a Non-Profit Organization that help women to break free from the poverty trap. Through its job-readiness training, career development, and job placement programs, B-Inspired.Org helps these women realize their full potential and achieve financial stability.

Yolanda grew up in Memphis, Tennessee and after traumatic experiences in her life, she was led by God to write her first book "Gracefully Broken," where she documents the lessons that she learned from her personal struggles and God's dealings in her life.

She is an upcoming author who connects with readers by sharing life experiences and Biblical principles that beautifully illustrate how God changes lives when people learn to trust Him, seek His will, and follow His lead, no matter their circumstances.

Yolanda is married to Mr. Vaughn Cowan and has one son Kenneth Washington, Jr. whom she both loves and adores. She has two sisters, her mother resides in Memphis and her father is deceased.

She fellowships at a church under an Apostolic Ministry and faithfully serves on the Teacher Ministry and is a member of the Women Group Life Ministry in her church. She regularly connects with her Christian sisters on a daily prayer line that helps them stay in touch through praying and intercession.

www.ingramcontent.com/pod-product-compliance
Lightning Source LLC
Chambersburg PA
CBHW070620300426
44113CB00010B/1598